Sacred Hunt

No Inuk ever said to me, "The hunt for seals is a sacred act," or words to that effect. The title of this book is meant, rather, to reflect the inescapable impression of a spiritual link between Inuit and seals, based on the stories and knowledge of the Inuit elders who informed this work. It is not the hunt alone, but the whole relationship—to which the hunt is central—that one might justly call sacred.

—D F P

Sacred Hunt

A PORTRAIT OF THE RELATIONSHIP BETWEEN SEALS AND INUIT

David F. Pelly

FOREWORD BY THE HONORABLE PETER IRNIQ

GREY STONE BOOKS
Douglas & McIntyre Publishing Group
Vancouver/Toronto

University of Washington Press
Seattle

Copyright © 2001 by David F. Pelly

01 02 03 04 05   5 4 3 2 1

Greystone Books
A division of Douglas & McIntyre Ltd.
2323 Quebec Street, Suite 201
Vancouver, British Columbia V5T 4S7
www.greystonebooks.com

NATIONAL LIBRARY OF CANADA
CATALOGUING IN PUBLICATION DATA

Pelly, David F. (David Fraser), 1948–
  Sacred hunt

  Includes bibliographical references and
index.
  ISBN 1-55054-885-9

  1. Inuit—Hunting. 2. Sealing—Arctic
regions. 3. Seals (animals)—Arctic
regions. I. Title.
E99.E7P4163 2001 306.3 C2001-910529-0

Editing by Nancy Flight
Jacket and text design by Val Speidel
Jacket photograph: Northwest Territories
Archives (N-1991-059-0244). Photo by Doug
Wilkinson.
Maps by Stuart Daniel
Printed and bound in Hong Kong
by C & C Offset Printing Co., Ltd.
Printed on acid-free paper ∞

Originated by Greystone Books and
published simultaneously in the
United States by the University of
Washington Press, PO Box 50096
Seattle, Washington 98145-5096

ISBN 0-295-98164-4

Last year the Canadian Mint used a design
by Germaine Arnatauyok (whose work
appears in this book) for the new two-
dollar coin, and she has recently published a
new collection of eighteen etchings, which
are available from galleries
specializing in Inuit art throughout
North America.

The publisher gratefully acknowledges the
support of the Canada Council and of
the British Columbia Ministry of Tourism,
Small Business and Culture. The publisher
also wishes to acknowledge the financial
support of the Government of Canada
through the Book Publishing Industry
Development Program (BPIDP) for its
publishing activities.

PAGE ii

Untitled (Man at the Seal
Hole), ca. 1955. Samissa
Passauralu Ivilla,
Puvirnituq, b. 1924. Stone,
24.2 x 20.3 x 23.5 cm.

Collection of The Winnipeg Art
Gallery; Bessie Bulman Collection;
gift of the Heirs of the Bessie Bulman
Estate (G-72-168). Photo by Ernest
Mayer, The Winnipeg Art Gallery.

PAGES vi–vii

An Inuit hunter, Karaluk, in
a sealskin kayak, Wrangell
Island, north of Chukotka,
Russia, 1914. Kenneth Gordon
Chipman collection, National Archives
of Canada (C71052). Photo by
W. L. McKinlay.

This work is dedicated, with gratitude and respect, to the many

Inuit who shared with me their Qaujimajatuqangit, *traditional*

knowledge and understanding, now recorded in these pages.

Perhaps by sharing, they have affirmed their profound

and lasting ownership of this knowledge.

CONTENTS

ℱOREWORD

I NUIT BELIEVE that there is only one *nattiq*. I am speaking about the seal that most non-Inuit call a ringed seal. We Inuit do not refer to other seals, such as the harp seal, harbor seal, or any other seal, as real "seals." The other seals each have a name of their own. Most of us don't even like to eat them.

In the early morning hours, shortly before dawn, my father used to literally pull me out of my nice warm *sinikvik* (caribou-skin sleeping bag). We would then travel by dog team over the sea ice to look for seals' *agluit* (breathing holes). My father, as an experienced Inuk hunter, always knew just what to do. I can still hear the heavy breathing of our dogs, with only an occasional bark, while we were seeking the *agluit*. There would be four of us: my father, my sister and her husband, and me, a young Inuk, learning the ways of a professional seal hunter. My father was a professional seal hunter. He knew everything about hunting.

In my homeland of Naujaat (Repulse Bay), Inuit used to go seal hunting in the month of *Nattiat* (the birth of seals), or March. March is a good time to hunt seals through the *agluit*. Inuit dogs were used to assist by sniffing for the seal holes. Inuit hunters would wait patiently for the seals to come up the holes, while others continued to look for seal holes. It was always guaranteed, where I come from, that seal holes would be on the east side of the ridges because the prevailing winds are always from the northwest, blowing to the east.

When I was a little boy, I remember my mother teaching my sister how to sew with sealskin materials. She would dry the sealskins in the summer or early fall. It was my responsibility to chew the newly dried sealskin to be used for the soles of boots; they were normally made out of *ugjuk* (bearded seal skin). The purpose of chewing these skins was to make them easy to sew for my mother and sister. My mother made the sealskin boots (*kamiit*) for my little brother, my father, and me and for herself, while my sister sewed for her husband and my nieces. Making the boots was indeed a lot of work. The *kamiit* my mother and my sister sewed were waterproof, needed for us to walk on the wet spring snow and on the wet moss on the land and for the rivers we had to cross. My mother and sister would make sealskin mitts and outer pants with the hair outside. Sealskin was good for clothing, especially for the rainy days in the springtime.

I can also remember my mother pounding seal fat inside the snow porch of our iglu. When she finished she would place the softened fat into the *qulliq* (Inuit oil lamp). The *qulliq* was our light and the source of heat for drying, cooking, and melting ice in the pot. We had seal fat only when there were seals around the area where we lived. If there were no seals, then there was no light. I can remember, as a child, times when there was no light.

When seals could not be found, Nuliajuk, a sea spirit, would be consulted. It is said that when Nuliajuk was mad, she would drive all the seals away from their usual breathing holes and on to others. Nuliajuk is the boss of all seals and other sea mammals. My father said this half-woman/half-fish would only be angry for some reason. Perhaps we did not perform all the spiritual practices required of us when we hunted. Both my father and brother-in-law always knew just what to do. Because each of them was an *angakkuq* (shaman), they would consult with Nuliajuk through their helping spirits and make peace with Nuliajuk. Then in the coming days there would be seals again in the area where we used to live. My father used to say that we must always show respect to the animals. He said that if you make fun of the animals, they will eventually pay you back.

When my father returned home with a seal, it was my mother's responsibility to butcher the animal. As soon as the seal was pulled through the entrance of our iglu, my mother would take her *ulu* (a moon-shaped, woman's knife), and get ready to skin the seal. Before she did that, she would take a small piece of freshwater ice and gently put it into the seal's mouth and let the dead seal drink water. She would then say, translated into English, "This is so that all seals under the ice will not go thirsty." How powerful and strong this simple message to the spirits was. And spirits listened!

I see a great need to protect, preserve, and promote our Inuit way of life. In this book you will discover that there is more to a seal than just popping up in a seal hole. You will learn about the Inuit world and its traditional lifestyle. Inuit Elders want our youth to know their ancestral knowledge but at the same time to get modern education and training. We want youth to get good jobs and be able to communicate in the world of modern technology. That is our wish for our youth in Nunavut.

My friend David Pelly has written this book about seals and has included things that have never been printed before. David has consulted with many Inuit from Nunavut and Nunavik while researching this book. He has listened to Inuit who still depend on these animals for their living and their clothing. Inuit have contributed much of their knowledge to this important book. You will learn something from David's work—he writes about the real stuff.

THE HONORABLE PETER IRNIQ
COMMISSIONER OF NUNAVUT

PREFACE

NETSER STOOD ATOP a mound of ice, more than doubling his height above the surface of the frozen ocean. This small mountain was a piece of early ice that had been turned on its side and then frozen in place six months earlier. High on his icy perch, Netser scanned the surface of the sea ice for seals and polar bears, two principal players in the natural drama of this Arctic world.

We were traveling across the sea ice on a spring hunting trip, our sleds pulled by snowmobiles. Several days earlier we had left Coral Harbour, an Inuit village on Southampton Island in the northwest corner of Hudson Bay. By now the rhythm of travel was second nature to all four members of the party, as we traversed mile after mile of snow and ice. On this day we were just short of reaching the Arctic Circle, headed north from Southampton Island across the ice of Frozen Strait. Our destination was the floe edge that Netser was sure would lie across the bottom of Foxe Basin, that great body of water south of the arcing back of Baffin Island.

On some parts of our journey, the sea ice seemed empty, void of life. On others, little black dots punctuated the world of white that surrounded us. There were hundreds of seals, basking in the sun's warmth beside the breathing holes that had kept them alive all winter long.

My Inuit companion on that trip nearly twenty years ago, Joe Netser, was a skilled hunter who knew the animals of his region well. Like many other hunters I have known across the North since then, he had the answers for most of my questions. But also like most hunters, he preferred showing to telling, and on this trip he showed me a great deal as we hunted for seals on the spring ice.

Standing atop his lookout that day on the sea ice, he spotted a tiny off-white speck in the distance, so obscure that even with binoculars I could not see it until he pointed it out. Netser assured me that

Bear-Seals-Pup Escaping Into Hole, Pelly Bay, 1987. Bernard Irqugaqtuq, 1918–1987. Ivory, antler, 2.5 x 8 x 3.3 cm. Eskimo Museum. Reprinted by permission of the Inuit Art Foundation.

it was a polar bear stealing toward a seal lying beside its hole. We approached warily, not wanting to disturb the natural course of events but eager to watch the drama unfold. The bear caught the seal—with a single claw through the seal's tail—and dispatched it efficiently with a deep bite at the neck. Rich, dark blood spurted out onto the ice, onto the bear's flank, and into the open circle of water in the seal's hole, through which the seal had vainly tried to escape.

In that death on the sea ice, seals came dramatically to life for me. Before this trip I knew seals from picture books, from zoos, and from media coverage of the controversy caused by Brigitte Bardot's visit to the sealing grounds off Newfoundland. I had no personal connection to seals. I had never eaten meat from a seal I had watched being killed. Although my life was centered in the Arctic at the time, I lived mostly inland among Caribou Inuit, who, without access to seals, generally did not favor seal meat. The remarkable process to which Netser had introduced me drove home the message that seals were at the very center of life in the Arctic, essential food for both humans and bears.

The massive white bear departed, leaving us to inspect the scene more carefully. She would surely return, said Netser, as he cut out the seal's rib cage for us to enjoy as lunch. "We'll leave the rest for her," he announced. "She's a better hunter than I'll ever be."

The man who showed me this snapshot of Arctic nature was named after the animal at the center of the drama. The universal

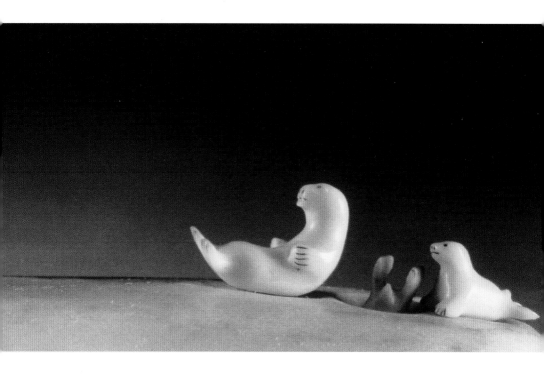

name that Inuit across all parts of the North use for the most common of seals in their waters, the ringed seal, is *natsiq* or *nattiq*, variously spelled and pronounced, depending on the local dialect. One of his grandfathers, Joe explained, had wanted him to understand the ways of the seal so that he would grow up to be a good hunter; that is why he was called Natsiq, which later was written down by a southern Canadian census taker as "Netser."

In the unending process of learning about the relationship between Inuit and seals, Netser was my first teacher; there have been many others since. The strength of this book, I hope, is that it is based directly on the traditional knowledge of the people whose lives depended on that knowledge.

When I was with Joe Netser high on the ice mound in Hudson Bay, searching the surface of the sea ice for seals and polar bears, I thought of these animals as the two principal players in the

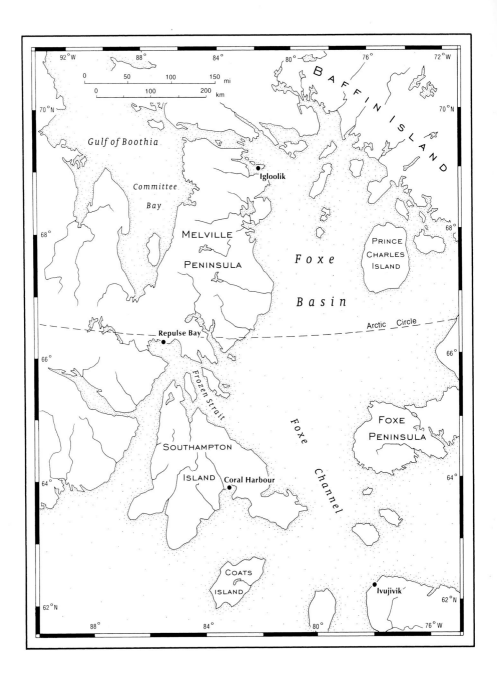

natural drama of this frozen world. Years later, my understanding has changed. I would now say that there are three principal players in that drama. The third is the indigenous people, who for centuries have depended upon the seals and who therefore have developed a profound understanding of, and respect for, the seals. In part, my newly acquired perspective reflects the Inuit world-view, wherein man and animals are equal partners in the ecosystem, neither one having any rights over the other. Netser, of course, offered me that perspective in his own way, but it took years of observation before I began to understand, before I realized what my friend Mikitok meant when he said he could communicate with the seals.

INTRODUCTION

DURING THE ICE AGE, most, if not all, of the circumpolar lands where people now live were covered by ice a kilometer or more thick. The end of the Ice Age, around ten thousand years ago, marks the beginning of the North as we know it today. As the ice retreated, scraping the land and filling the oceans, the map of today began to take shape. Relieved of the great weight of ice, the land gradually rebounded, rising out of the sea. Soil slowly began to develop, eventually allowing vegetation to grow. So too abundant life returned to the waters of the Arctic from the seas farther south that had remained unfrozen.

Sometime later humans arrived on the Arctic coasts of Europe, Asia, North America, and Greenland. There they found a group of mammals ideally suited to their needs: seals. The seals were large enough to be worth the effort of the hunt and yet not so large as to present excessive difficulty or danger. Not only did they provide food, their skin became a leather that was both waterproof and warm, and their blubber could be rendered into fuel. The seal soon became the principal prey of the newly settled circumpolar peoples, essential for their survival.

Eight species of seals are found in Arctic waters, but only two are true Arctic seals—full-time, year-round residents.

Ringed seals are found throughout the Arctic. About 100,000 of them are still harvested every year by Inuit in Canada and Greenland. How many exist remains a mystery because they spend so much of the time underwater, even under the frozen surface of the Arctic Ocean, surviving by rising to breathe from the breathing holes they make in the 2-meter-thick ice. Estimates of the world population of ringed seals range from two million to as high as ten million. The common name in English comes from the abundance of ringed markings on the mature seal's pelt. To the Sami, these seals are *gette.* In Russian they are *akiba;* along parts of the northern coast of Russia they have been harvested by indigenous people for centuries. And to Inuit, they are *nattiq. Nattiq* is the fundamental food of Inuit from Chukotka in the northeast corner of Russia, over the Bering Strait to Alaska, across the top of Canada, and east to Greenland. All Inuit share both the word and the strong connection to this animal above all others.

Many of the much larger bearded seals, the other truly Arctic seal, also remain under the Arctic ice all winter, but they prefer floating pack ice to solid, land-fast ice. They too are capable of making and maintaining breathing holes in the solid ice, however. The total circumpolar population of bearded seals probably exceeds one million animals, but there has been so little study of the bearded seal that no accurate estimates exist. The common name in English derives from the tufts of long whiskers pointing downward on either side of the snout, which probably help the seal to find its food on the ocean floor. Another English name used through much of Canada is "square flipper," a translation of what Norwegian sealers used to call the bearded seal. The Sami call these seals *aine,* the same name that they use for the gray seal. In western Russia the term is *morski zaits,* referring to the manner in which the bearded seal appears to leap into the water from the ice when alarmed. Farther east in Russia, the name for the bearded seal is *lachtak.* Among the Yupik of southwest Alaska it is *mukluk,* also the well-known term for some types of skin boots. From the Chukotkan shore of the Bering Strait, across to northern Alaska, through Canada, and over to Greenland, the seal's name is *ugjuk* or *ussuk* or a similar rendering of the same word.

Another seal that was important for the survival of indigenous peoples in the Arctic was the harp seal, so named because of the

FACING PAGE

The circumpolar world.

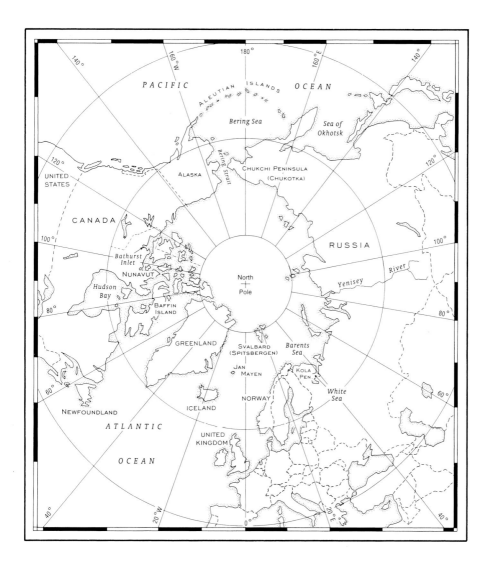

black saddle, which somewhat resembles a harp, on the pelt of the adult. To the circumpolar peoples, harp seals are known as *aataaq* (Greenlandic), *daelja* (Sami), and *qairulik* (Inuit). There are three populations of harp seals in the circumpolar world. The largest, which numbers about five million seals and has been stable in recent years, lives in the northwest Atlantic, breeding on the ice off Canada's east coast in March every year, where the photogenic "whitecoats" are born, and then heading north up the Labrador coast as spring advances. These are the seals made famous in the 1970s and early '80s by the controversy surrounding the annual hunt by Newfoundland and Magdalen Islands sealers. And these are the harp seals that Inuit have been hunting for generations on the west coast of Greenland, as have the Inuit of Baffin Island.

On Greenland's east coast, a second population of about a quarter million harp seals gives birth in the spring on the ice between Jan Mayen and Svalbard (Spitsbergen). A third population of uncertain size ranges throughout the waters north of Norway in the Barents Sea and to the east along the coast of Russia and congregates annually for whelping on the pack ice of the White Sea, a few weeks earlier than their counterparts off Newfoundland.

Another Arctic seal, the ribbon seal, found in the Bering and Chukchi Seas, was not essential to indigenous people. It is such an extraordinary-looking seal, however, with its highly contrasted stripes, that some Inuit hunted it just for the aesthetic value of its pelt. Among coastal Inuit of both Chukotka and Alaska, it was once popular to use the decoratively colored pelt of the ribbon seal to make a bag to hold their sealskin clothing.

Harbor seals, spotted seals, hooded seals, and gray seals are all regular visitors to northern waters, and all have been used incidentally by indigenous people, but none of them were essential to their

survival. The three main seals—ringed, bearded, and harp—were capable of fulfilling all the peoples' needs.

Although Inuit were the only indigenous people so profoundly dependent on seals, others in the circumpolar world also made use of the resource in important ways.

The coast of Iceland is dotted with place names that reflect the people's use of seals, beginning when Norse settlers arrived in the 9th century—for example, Seley ("seal island"), Kópavogur ("bay

Hunting Scenes by **Twammie (Tommy) Okaituk.** Reproduced by permission of the artist and of La Fédération des Coopératives du Nouveau-Québec.

of baby seals"), and Urtusteinn ("female seal rock"). Records show that in the 1600s there were 364 seal-hunting farms, where coastal landowners exercised their right to net, club, harpoon, or shoot seals in the waters just offshore. Historically, the oil was used for lamps and consumed for health reasons, the skin was used as leather, and the meat formed a significant part of the Icelandic diet. In the Middle Ages, the famous Icelandic saga manuscripts were bound in sealskin.

Although the Sami of northern Norway are best known for their dependence on reindeer, they also harvested seals on the coast to supplement their food supply and to acquire the extremely useful skins, which were more durable and waterproof than the reindeer hides. In Russia, the Nenets, who occupy the coastal and inland area immediately east of the White Sea to the Yenisey River, followed a way of life much like that of the Sami; although seals were not of critical importance, they were used by those with ready access to the sea. Along the central Siberian coast, there is no evidence of substantial indigenous use of seals. But in the northeast corner of Russia, several distinct groups of indigenous peoples made regular use of seals: the Even, the Koryak, the Chukchi, and the Yupik. In many respects, their way of life, dependence on marine mammals, and hunting methods were similar to those of Inuit farther east in North America. The Russian Yupik, historically, are immediate cousins of some Alaskan Inuit living just across the Bering Strait.

People in the Arctic may even have used seals before the last ice age ended. There is a theory that the Sami people lived along the northern coast of Scandinavia *during* the Ice Age, that a thin margin of land remained uncovered by ice. If that was so, and other theories about the origins of the Sami are incorrect, then undoubtedly the people survived largely by hunting and fishing in the ice-covered sea, and no animal would have been more vital to their survival than the seal.

At least four thousand years ago, considerably before any ancestors of modern-day fair-haired, blue-eyed Norwegians or Swedes arrived, there was a substantial population of indigenous peoples—calling themselves the Samek—living in the vast region stretching across the northern half of today's Norway, Sweden, and Finland and into Russia where the Kola Peninsula extends into the White Sea. Measured along the coast, the extent of this area exceeds 2000 kilometers, not including the many fjords of the Norwegian coast, which would surely double that figure. Today, a Sami population of approximately sixty thousand still occupies that territory—which they call Sapmi, without regard for the political borders it crosses.

The Sami, formerly called Lapps by others but not by themselves, lived in diverse ways as dictated by their local environment. Many were chiefly dependent on hunting in the forests and mountains of the interior. A few developed farming techniques; the domestication of reindeer is a relatively recent phenomenon. But some, mainly in what is now Norway, relied to a great extent on the sea. These coastal Sami were less nomadic than their inland cousins, retreating only as far as the heads of the fjords for the winter but retaining their attachment to the sea throughout the year. They built boats, mostly from wood, which they used for fishing and seal hunting. Armed with harpoons much like those used elsewhere around the circumpolar world, they hunted from their boats for both ringed and harp seals. The meat was an important source of food. The sealskin was used for waterproof boots and clothing and for rope, all of which was also exchanged with other

Making a kayak, Quebec, 1874. Notman Photographic Archives, McCord Museum of Canadian History, Montreal (MP-0000.391.12).

Sami based in the interior and, more recently, with newly arrived Norwegians from the south. A few hundred years ago, as those new arrivals began to dominate the fjords, many Sami moved inland and abandoned their former way of life focused on the sea. Those that remained were largely acculturated into the dominant society, and the way of life of the coastal Sami all but disappeared about a century ago.

Whether the Sami people were in the Arctic during the Ice Age or arrived shortly after deglaciation, they were among the first of today's circumpolar peoples to discover the uses of seals in the Arctic. But exactly when that occurred remains uncertain.

In northern Europe, there is evidence that neolithic people

hunted seals; harpoon heads best suited for seal hunting have been found at several archeological sites. A rock engraving in northern Norway depicts a man in a boat pursuing a seal, suggesting a hunting scene. The methods of these early people were probably not that much different from those developed to a much greater level of sophistication, and used even more recently, by Inuit from Chukotka and Alaska across Canada to Greenland. Many of these technologies survive even today, somewhat adapted to modern materials, but nevertheless requiring the same skills and knowledge of the prey as in the past.

The way in which Inuit and their predecessors have used these seals for the past four thousand years is closely tied to the life cycle of the seal itself. These people and seals live in much the same environment; neither has sought to leave. Both view the sea ice as a welcome feature of the severe Arctic climate. And both have developed heightened sensitivities to the environment they share. This point was brought home to me at a community gathering in Cambridge Bay, 300 kilometers north of the Arctic Circle, one day in late March. An Inuit elder, Analok, stood at the window, looking outside. He pointed out the sun, which had a rainbow-colored parhelic ring around it, referred to in the North as a sun dog, and said matter-of-factly: "When we see that, we know the *nattiq* is about to give birth." For this old Inuit man, the natural phenomena of the Arctic were all bound together in the cycle of life as he had known it, and at the center of it all was the birth of more seals.

Respect for the Seal

I have always hunted for seals. I really enjoy seals.
We do not play around with animals. We respect
animals. We kill it as quickly as possible. This is how
we do it. We appreciate the animals. We hunt for them.

Lᴜᴄᴀssɪᴇ Kᴀᴛᴛᴜᴋ, ʙᴏʀɴ 1928, Sᴀɴɪᴋɪʟᴜᴀǫ, Nᴜɴᴀᴠᴜᴛ

The Creation of Seals

Lᴏɴɢ ᴀɢᴏ, there lived in the Arctic a young and beautiful woman. Many men were presented to her as prospective husbands, but she rejected them all, until one day a handsome stranger came to her family's camp. He had many dogs and finely crafted hunting tools, and he promised her a life of comfort. She could not resist, and she left with him for his land across the sea, only to find on her arrival that she had been deceived. Her betrothed was in fact a seabird, and his dwelling was a hovel.

When her father came to rescue her, they escaped in his boat across the calm sea. But her seabird husband's spirit, angered by this, pursued them and whipped the icy sea into a raging storm. In midocean in a small boat, the father feared for his life and, to appease the bird, cast his daughter overboard into the wave-tossed waters. But she clung relentlessly to the gunwale of his boat. Determined to release her grip, the father cut off her fingers at the first knuckle; the pieces fell into the sea and became ringed seals. Still she held on. Then he cut all her fingers at the second joint, and those pieces swam away as bearded seals. Other pieces of her fingers became walruses and whales.

That is how seals were created, and that young woman became Nuliajuk, the Mother of the Sea, also known as Sedna, Taleelayu, Niviaqsi, Arnakapsaaluk, Takanakapsaaluk, Takanaluk arnaluk,

FACING PAGE

Shaman Summoning Taleelayuk to Release Animals, 1989. Manasie Akpaliapik, Arctic Bay, b. 1955. Whalebone, narwhal ivory, 43.7 x 40.2 x 27.8 cm. Collection of The Winnipeg Art Gallery; acquired with funds from The Winnipeg Art Gallery Foundation Inc. (G-90-506). Photo by Ernest Mayer, The Winnipeg Art Gallery.

OVERLEAF

Sedna, Sea Goddess, 1994, etching. Germaine **Arnaktauyok**. Collection of The Winnipeg Art Gallery; acquired with the support of the Canada Council for the Arts Acquisition Assistance program and with funds from The Winnipeg Art Gallery Foundation Inc.

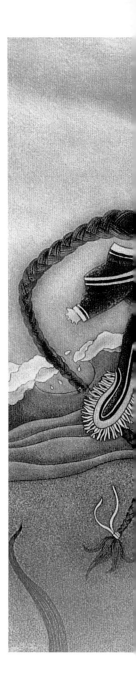

Nirrivik, Uinigumisuitung, and Anavigak. To this day, she lives at the bottom of the sea and controls all the animals in her watery domain.

The creation of the seals was of profound importance to Inuit. The seals became a lifeline, the very means of survival for the people. From the beginning, Inuit had a deep respect for the seals, and this respect forms the basis of their relationship with the seals.

Transformation

LIKE ALL PEOPLE and animals long ago, Inuit and seals spoke the same language and lived in absolute harmony, as equal partners in the natural world. Animals could also reason and react to events in much the same way as humans, and they were capable of human-like emotions. When it suited them, hunters could turn themselves into animals, and animals could become human beings. Inuit tell stories of human beings transformed into seals and of seals being transformed into human beings. So too a seal could become a caribou or a fox. All creatures were equal in this regard, including humans.

⌒ PEOPLE AND ANIMALS COULD TALK

In the beginning animals did communicate with people. It was told that in the beginning of first man, every living creature spoke, including humans, caribou, lemmings, mosquitoes . . .

GEORGE KUPTANA, BORN 1914, BATHURST INLET, NUNAVUT
TRANSLATED BY JOHN NANEGOAK, COLLECTED BY DOUG STERN

⌒ A STORY OF TRANSFORMATION

A *man who had been out seal hunting for the whole day was walking in the evening going home. He started to see another Inuk ahead of him, in the direction he was walking. It was all ice where he was walking, and down toward the end where the ice was rough, he saw the Inuk. It looked like he was coming out of something on the path where the hunter would be walking. So he decided to continue walking to pass by this Inuk. This Inuk seemed to be coming out, although there was no iglu in sight, near the edge of an area of rough ice. And then, when the hunter arrived to the Inuk, and met him, he saw that the Inuk had very short legs for a human being. I suppose the hunter did not think he arrived to some Inuit people. He met the Inuk near his doorway, he was told by the Inuk who just stepped out of his doorway, "You are asked to enter, for there is a complicated birth about to happen." The short-legged Inuk told him this. This Inuk was strange, although it looked like a human being.*

The hunter did not go into the house; he must have been frightened by what he saw, although he understood the Inuk when he spoke. The hunter continued on walking. His mind found the Inuk strange. Perhaps, even if he had gone inside, he would have been afraid. This Inuk was very different, with such short legs. Then, when the hunter was at a distance, because he did not go in, the short-legged Inuk shouted to him: "You will never catch seals any more, because you did not say Yes! You will not catch seals any more." But this did not make him turn back to go into the iglu. And it was true that he never caught seals again, as he had been told by the short-legged Inuk. This was a seal that had turned into a human being. Animals used to turn into human beings.

QUPIRRUALUK, 83, PUVIRNITUQ, QUEBEC
TRANSLATED BY QILUQQI

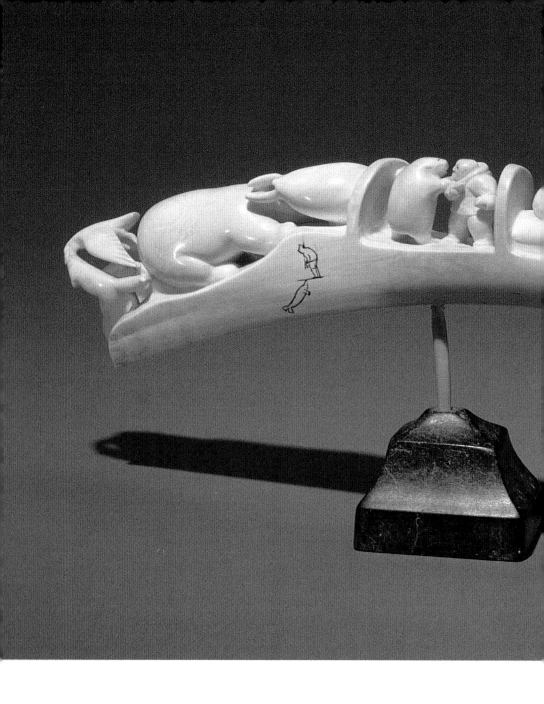

⌒ THE SEAL AND THE WOLF

Once the wolf met a seal on the ice, both having the forms of men at the time. The wolf said to the seal, "Whenever an arrow is shot at me I jump quickly to one side and it misses." The seal answered, "I too, whenever a harpoon is hurled at me, dodge to one side." The wolf retorted, "I can jump out of the way more quickly than you." So the seal took a bow and shot three arrows in succession, which struck and killed the wolf. Then the seal put on its seal-coat and dived into the water.

ILATSIAQ, COLLECTED BY DIAMOND JENNESS, 1916

From the northwest corner of Alaska to the shores of Hudson Bay in eastern Canada, beliefs about transformation were much the same. Half a world away, old Norse mythology offers many variations on the same theme. In Shetland, the islands north of Scotland originally settled by Norsemen—at about the same latitude as the Inuit community of Arviat on the Hudson Bay coast, or of Great Slave Lake in the Northwest Territories—a man stabbed a large seal he found sleeping on the rocks by the shore. The seal escaped with the man's knife stuck in his thick skin. Later, the Shetlander went to visit an old friend on the west coast of Norway, and the friend asked whether the Shetlander had lost a knife. The Shetlander told his story of the seal that escaped, whereupon the old man showed him a knife, which the Shetlander immediately recognized as the one he had lost.

"It would not have been so bad if you had not twisted the knife when you put it in," said the old man, revealing to his friend for the first time that he was one of the people who could take on the form of a large seal. In some versions of the story, he shows a wound to

FACING PAGE

Takannaluk, 1994, drawing. Germaine Arnaktauyok. Collection of The Winnipeg Art Gallery; acquired with the support of the Canada Council for the Arts Acquisition Assistance program and with funds from The Winnipeg Art Gallery Foundation Inc.

his visitor in the very spot where the knife had penetrated the seal.

These men with the magical power to become large seals could also foretell the future, control the weather, commune with other animals, and travel exceedingly fast, and in many other ways resembled the Inuit shamans of the era before the Europeans arrived.

Seals could also transform themselves into people, most often women, called Selkies. Stories in Norway, Shetland, Orkney, the Faroes, and Iceland tell of seals coming ashore, removing their skins, and dancing happily in unclothed human form. The stories

vary slightly from one island to the next as you move farther and farther offshore from Viking origins in Norway, but the central theme is the same. A man sees one of the dancing figures, falls in love, and takes the seal-woman as his wife. Some years later, having borne his children, she escapes and returns to the sea. Today on any of these islands you can find people who have what the locals call "a thick horny skin" on the palms of their hands and the soles of their feet, enough to identify them as descendants of the Selkies who married local men.

The ability of seals and people to transform into each other and to intermarry suggests a relationship of equity and respect, and for Inuit this relationship extended to the hunt. Inuit have traditionally believed that their attitude toward seals is the key to whether they will be successful in the hunt. If they approach the seal in a respectful manner, it will not object to being caught and the hunt will be successful. If the seal is mistreated in any way, it will not give itself to the hunter. Or if the seal is caught, the spirit released from the dead animal will tell other animals, who will then avoid the offending hunter and other hunters from his camp and not allow themselves to be caught. When that happens, Inuit have to observe certain rituals and taboos to cajole the animals into cooperating and once again offering themselves to the hunter.

FACING PAGE

In mythologies all around the circumpolar world, seals could become beautiful young women. *Sea Goddess*, 1997, Annie Michael, Kimmirut. Green stone, 16.5 x 30.0 x 23.5 cm. National Gallery of Canada; gift of Dorothy M. Stillwell. Reprinted by permission of Public Trustee for Nunavut, estate of Annie Michael (29110).

⌒ THE NORSE SEAL-WIFE

Seals originally came from people who jumped from cliffs or drowned themselves in the sea. Once every year, on Twelfth Night, they are able to take off their skins and are then like other people; then they enjoy themselves by dancing and playing in human manner on the flat rocks by the shore or inside the seal-caverns.

The story goes that a young man of South Farm in Mikladalur heard how the seals used to assemble on Twelfth Night in a cavern not far from the village. He went that evening to find out whether what was said about this was true or not. He hid himself behind a boulder near the mouth of the cave. After sunset he saw great numbers of seals come swimming there; when they came ashore, they took off their skins and put them on the flat rocks by the shore, and now they were in every way like other folk.

The young man of Mikladalur was very pleased to watch from behind the rock where he lay. Now he saw an extremely fine and beautiful maiden come from one sealskin. He at once fell in love with her, and he noticed very carefully where she put her skin not far from him. The young man now crept up, took the skin and then once again hid behind the boulder.

The seals danced and made merry all night; but when day began to break, each one went back for his skin. But the seal-maiden who was mentioned before could not find her skin, and walked about searching for it with wailing and pitiful lamentation, for the night was gone and the sun would soon be rising. But before the sun rose from the sea, she caught the scent of her skin with the Mikladalur man, and asked him for it. She implored him with the most touching words to give her back the skin, but he would not listen to her and went up the steep track to his house, and she had to follow him for the skin he carried with him.

He now took her as his wife and they lived happily with each other like other couples. But always he had to be careful not to let her get at the skin; he thus kept it in a chest, securely locked, and he always had the key upon him.

One day he was out fishing, and as he sat there out on the sea and pulled in a fish, his hand happened to touch his belt, where the key used to hang. He was thunderstruck, for only now did he realize that the key was left behind, and in sadness and sorrow he cried out, "Today I have lost my wife!" They all drew up their lines, put out their oars, and rowed home as swiftly as possible. When the Mikladalur man came to his house, he saw that his wife had gone, but that the children the two of them had had remained quietly in the house. So that they should come to no harm while they were indoors alone, she had put out the fire in the house, and set all the knives and other sharp things under lock and key. When she had done this, she had run down to the shore, put on the skin and thrown herself into the sea. She had found the key when her husband was out fishing, opened up the chest and seen where her skin was lying. Then she could restrain herself no longer, from whence comes the saying "could no more control herself than a seal when it sees its skin." The moment she leapt into the sea, the bull seal, who earlier had been in love with her, came to her side, and the two now swam away; all these years he had been waiting for her. When the children she had had with the Mikladalur man came down to the shore, a seal could be seen swimming off-shore looking at them, and everyone thought this must be the seal-wife.

Many years now passed, in which nothing more is to be told of the farmer of South Farm or the seal-wife's children. But then one day the Mikladalur men decided to go to the breeding-caverns to kill seals; and the night before, the seal-wife came to the farmer in a dream, and told him that if he went to the caves with the others, he should take care

that they did not kill the bull seal that would be waiting at the mouth
of the cave, for that was her mate, and they must spare the two seal-
pups that were lying innermost in the cavern, for they were their sons,
and she described their colouring. But the farmer paid no heed to this
dream; he went with the Mikladalur men to the cave, and they killed
all the seals that were in there. When the catch was divided, the farmer
got as his share the whole bull seal, and the flippers and tails of the
pups. For supper they boiled the head, flippers and tails, and when they
were served up, a great noise and commotion was heard, and the seal-
wife entered the living room like the ugliest of trolls, sniffed in the dish
and cried out angrily, "Here lies the old one with the upturned nose, the
hand of Hàrek and the foot of Fridrik vengeance now and in time to
come shall be upon the Mikladalur men; some shall be drowned, and
some shall fall from the cliffs; and this shall continue, until as many
have been lost as could link arms round the whole island of Kalsoy."
When she had said this, she went out again with noise and rumbling,
and was seen no more.

FROM *Faroese folk-tales & legends*, by John F. West

FACING PAGE

Sedna with a Hairbrush,
1985, Natar Ungalaq,
Igloolik. Stone, fur, bone,
18.0 x 21.5 x 20.0 cm.

National Gallery of Canada

(3256.1-2).

Rituals and Taboos

WHEN A HUNT was successful, it was due to the benevolence of
Nuliajuk, the Mother of the Sea. But she was vindictive when traditional customs were neglected. She might cause a storm to prevent the hunters from going to sea, or break the ice and drown
them. Or she might simply keep her seals to herself. It was said that
she was most happy when her hair was tidy, but she had no fingers
with which to comb it. So when her hair became figuratively tangled with the misdemeanors of Inuit, and her anger led to a decline
in the number of her animals released to the hunters, the shaman
had to pay a visit to her dwelling on the sea bottom. He had to
comb her hair and thereby pacify the Mother of the Sea so that she
would release the seals to the hunters.

The shamans were called upon in different ways to ensure the
success of the hunt, and thus the survival of their people. It was the
shamans who could communicate with the spirit world, and it was
up to the shamans to exercise the respect people needed to show in
order to have a successful hunt. If someone in camp stepped outside of the bounds of appropriate conduct, the shaman imposed a
taboo to avoid ill consequence. He could order that person not to
eat meat directly off the bone, insisting that it be cut away first as
an act of contrition. He would always insist that the meat of sea
mammals and the meat of land mammals not be mixed, either in
the cooking pot or on the storage platform in the iglu. If these
strict rules were not obeyed, the group as a whole would surely be
punished with a less successful hunt.

⌒ ABIDING BY THE RULES

People had a certain way of life that they lived and had to follow the rules of the day. This was the only way that they were able to live harmoniously with their surroundings. That was the way it was for them. It was necessary for them to abide by the rules in their lives. If they were to breach any rules then there was always the danger that it would affect their daily life, so they had strict rules that they had to follow. They feared for their life when rules were breached in any way.

HUBERT AMARUALIK, 75, IGLOOLIK, NUNAVUT
TRANSLATED BY LOUIS TAPARDJUK,
IGLOOLIK INULLARIIT ELDERS SOCIETY,
IGLOOLIK RESEARCH CENTRE (IE023)

Alive and free, alive but on the end of a harpoon, lying dead on the ice, or butchered into meat back at the camp, the seal was always respected by the hunter and others in his camp. Respect was the key to a successful hunt, and a successful hunt was the essence of survival. In this way, for Inuit, respect lies at the center of the struggle to exist as a hunting culture. Respect for each other, in particular for one's elders, and respect for the animals who provide one's food remain the basic tenets of Inuit life today.

⌒ RESPECT TOWARD
THE SEALS

Inuit were extremely respectful toward seals. My father used to catch a seal and put it into our iglu. Before my mother skinned the seal, she would put a piece of ice in her own mouth to melt, then let the meltwater fall into the dead seal's mouth. She said this was to make sure that the seals under the ice will not be thirsty. She did this every time. It's a spiritual belief, done out of respect for the seals.

<small>Peter Irniq, born 1947, Repulse Bay, Nunavut</small>

Men and Seals, 1981.
Simon Hiqiniq, Gjoa
Haven. Light green stone,
21.6 x 26.3 x 14.1 cm.

National Gallery of Canada; gift of

Dorothy M. Stillwell (29124).

Respect for the Seal 29

⌒ STORY FROM THE INUPIAT OF NORTHERN ALASKA

A *man was hunting seals. He heard two of them talking. One said to the other, "Go over to where that man sits and come up through the* aglu." *But the other said, "No, he will catch me and when he does, he will drag me home and bump my head on the ice." But the first seal said, "His wife will be sharpening her ulu [knife] all the time; why don't you go over there?" They stopped talking and the second came up though the* aglu *[breathing hole] and the man caught it. On the way home, he was careful not to bump its head on the ice. At home he told his wife to give the seal a drink of fresh water. He made her sharpen her ulu carefully and advised her not to stir the seal meat in the pot. After that, the man and his wife were careful to observe this way of treating seals and [he] was able to catch a great many.*

FROM SPENCER, The North Alaskan Eskimo, P. 267

⌒ SOULS

All *the creatures that we have to kill and eat, all those that we have to strike down and destroy to make clothes for ourselves, have souls, like we have, souls that do not perish with the body, and which must therefore be propitiated lest they should revenge themselves on us for taking away their bodies.*

Ivaluardjuk, collected by Knud Rasmussen, 1922

FACING PAGE

Seal with Spirit Helper,
1960–1965. **David Ruben
Piqtoukun, Cape Dorset, b.
1937. Stone, 18.5 x 26.9 x
8.9 cm.** Collection of The Winnipeg

Art Gallery; acquired with funds pro-

vided by The Winnipeg Art Gallery

Foundation Inc. (G-88-357).

Hunting the Seal

*This is the way we have always existed, using seals.
I don't think our ancestors would have survived if there
had been no seals.*

JOHNNY MEEKO SR., BORN 1935, SANIKILUAQ, NUNAVUT

Johnny Meeko Sr.

The *Mauliq* Hunt in Winter

*During the long winter months, when daylight was short
and the winds were howling, there was great hardship.*

FRANK ANALOK, 82, CAMBRIDGE BAY, NUNAVUT

DAWN HAS NOT yet broken over the small cluster of iglus on the vast plain of ice. Inside, lying beneath their caribou-skin robes, the hunters awake while it is still dark. They sit on the edge of their sleeping platforms and quickly dress. The air inside the iglus is so frigid that they can see their breath as they speak. Will the weather today permit a hunt?

In this scene from the early 20th century, in a winter camp high in the Arctic, ten Inuit families have cast their fates together in the struggle to survive. There are about a hundred people in the camp —more than in the less-well-off groups, those with no dogs and less of the equipment necessary for travel and the hunt. More hunters means a better chance of success and survival. They are living life on the edge, for there is no excess of food here. Their families' survival depends on their success at the seal hunt.

Sometime before the winter solstice, once the sea ice was solid and enough snow had accumulated to enable them to build iglus, the families left their camps on the land and moved onto the ice,

FACING PAGE

**An Inuit camp on the sea
ice in the western Canadian
Arctic, ca. 1915.** Diamond
Jenness Collection, Canadian Museum
of Civilization (51168).

33

Hunting the Seal   35

taking with them only the barest necessities. The lucky ones had a dog team to pull their loaded sleds. Many carried all their possessions on their backs: the caribou skins to keep them warm, the soapstone oil lamp, or *qulliq,* to heat and light the iglu, and the winter seal-hunting tools that had been readied over the preceding months.

Now the most difficult phase of life in the Arctic is beginning. Windswept and barren, the sea ice will be the people's home and their principal hunting ground for half the year. For several months there will be very little light, sometimes only twilight, by which to travel and hunt.

⌒ MOVING TO THE SEA ICE FOR WINTER

As winter was approaching, the Inuit would head out to the sea to spend their long winters there to hunt for seals. They pulled their own loads of belongings because dogs were not many then. . . . They never had trouble pulling their sleds because they helped one another. That was how they lived.

When the sea ice had frozen over, they headed towards their wintering spot. They helped and shared amongst themselves. Every winter they went to the sea ice. It had been done in the past and they followed what their parents and grandparents did before them. This was what their ancestors did. They looked to the sea to provide seal oil for heating and cooking because in the land you cannot find oil for heat.

MOSES KOIHOK, BORN 1921, BATHURST INLET, NUNAVUT
TRANSLATED BY TOMMY KILAODLUK, COLLECTED BY DOUG STERN

ABOVE

Several families traveling to their winter camp, western Canadian Arctic, ca. 1915. Diamond Jenness Collection, Canadian Museum of Civilization (37103).

FACING PAGE

A family heads out onto the sea ice in early winter to establish their seal-hunting camp, Coronation Gulf, western Canadian Arctic, ca. 1915. Diamond Jenness Collection, Canadian Museum of Civilization (37028).

Winds of 30 kilometers an hour are normal, and winds of 50 kilometers an hour are not unusual. The temperature often remains at −40° for days on end. The windchill factor will often plummet to −60°C. Some days, when whiteouts threaten one's very survival, the hunters rest, perform small maintenance tasks on their equipment, and spend time with their families, secure inside the thick, protective snow walls of the iglu. Most of the time, the families are hungry and have little blubber to burn in the lamps.

On this day the weather is clear. The hunters will go out in search of the ringed seal, *nattiq*, the linchpin in the traditional Inuit struggle to survive in much of the circumpolar world. Ringed seals do not go very far offshore, rarely more than 20 kilometers in open water. Ice, particularly shore-fast ice, is their favored domain for much of the year. They especially like the ice edge, where an abundance of food attracts a great deal of marine life. Perhaps most remarkable of all, in winter ringed seals remain under the ice cover of the frozen Arctic Ocean, obtaining the air they need to survive by making and maintaining a system of breathing holes through the thick Arctic ice.

At the onset of freeze-up, the seals use the cracks running for great distances across the ice to obtain the air they need to survive. Eventually, however, most of the cracks freeze over, and as they do, the seals continue to make small holes through the relatively thin ice so that they can breathe. They rise to the underside of the ice and blow out, pushing the ice up into a small dome and leaving a breathing hole, or *aglu* (plural: *agluit*), no larger than the tip of your thumb. They swim under the ever-thickening ice from one hole to the next to the next in turn, keeping them open, at first by cracking the ice with their heads and then by gnawing and scraping at the ice as it thickens around the initial hole. It is these holes

that the hunters look for. In the winter hunt, called *mauliq*, the hunters wait for the seals to appear at their breathing holes and strike them with their harpoons as the animals rise to the surface to take a breath.

⌒ CAMPING ON THE SEA ICE

I remember camping in the winter season out on the frozen sea ice. As a child, during the winter, the people never stayed on the land. When winter came, the people moved out on the ice. For the winter, the people would build a large snowhouse with a big workspace in the center. From the sides, they would build tunnels. And at the end of each tunnel, a family would build their living quarters. The center was a workspace or a place to gather for games, drum dances, and stories. That was repeated each year.

RUTH NIGIYONAK, BORN 1899, HOLMAN, NORTHWEST TERRITORIES

On this early winter morning, the hunters dress by the light of their *qulliq*, pulling on their warm caribou-skin clothing, which their wives made at their camp on land before the family moved out onto the sea ice for the winter. Out of respect for the animals, the products of land mammals and those of sea mammals must be kept separate. Because the ice is the domain of sea mammals, the caribou-skin clothing to be worn while seal hunting out on the ice must be made on land. In the same way, a pot used for cooking caribou meat is not to be used for cooking seal, and any tools soiled with caribou blood are not to be used on seals.

The hunters put on caribou-skin parkas, the warmest coat there

PREVIOUS PAGE

A winter camp in northern Quebec, ca. 1910 Notman Photographic Archives, McCord Museum of Canadian History, Montreal (MP-1976.26.50).

FACING PAGE

Seal Hunter with a Harpoon, **1994, drawing, Germaine Arnaktauyok.** Collection of The Winnipeg Art Gallery; acquired with the support of the Canada Council for the Arts Acquisition Assistance program and with funds from The Winnipeg Art Gallery Foundation Inc.

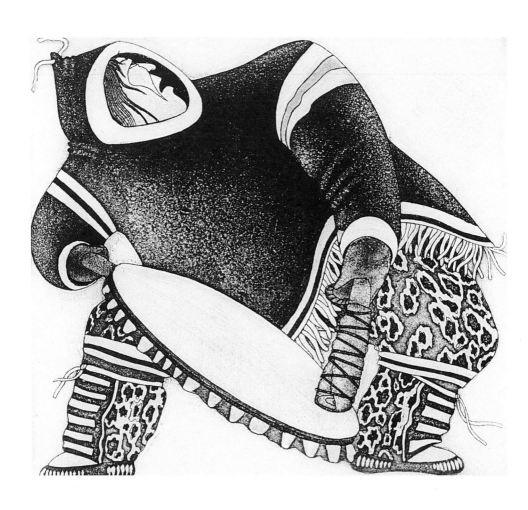

is, made from the thick hides of the autumn caribou. Their pants and mittens, too, are made from caribou skin, but their boots might be made of either caribou or sealskin, which is waterproof.

To improve his chances at the hunt, by ensuring that the seals' souls are positively disposed toward him, a hunter might carry the teeth of an Arctic fox, or a sea scorpion might be sewn into the back of his inner coat. Teeth from a seal he has caught might be sewn onto the outside of the inner coat in front of each breast, or the claws and the skin of the head of a seal he has caught might be sewn onto the back of the neck of the inner coat. All of these amulets will bring the hunter good luck.

Each hunter carries an *unaaq,* or harpoon; some tools for probing the snow and feeling the size and shape of the seal's breathing holes; a shoulder bag containing his *naulaq,* or harpoon head (also called *sakku* and *tuukaq*); a sealskin pull-rope for dragging the seal home across the ice; and a knife. He would also carry a snowknife, and he might have an indicator that he will set up in a breathing hole to warn him that the seal is rising toward the surface. This could be as simple as a swan's feather stuck in the snow above the *aglu* so that it will move when a seal pushes water and air upward as it rises to breathe. Or it could be a more sophisticated indicator ornately carved in bone. Sometimes, especially if it's so cold that the top of the *aglu* freezes over very quickly, the hunter will insert a thin bone rod down into the hole so that it rises as the seal approaches. At an open-water *aglu* a hunter might suspend a line made of caribou sinew into the hole, with a tiny piece of down just above the surface, so that its vibration will alert the hunter to the rising seal.

FACING PAGE

Drummer, 1993, etching, Germaine Arnaktauyok.

Collection of The Winnipeg Art Gallery; acquired with the support of the Canada Council for the Arts Acquisition Assistance program and with funds from The Winnipeg Art Gallery Foundation Inc.

BELOW

Seal amulets carved in ivory by Tuniit (Dorset Eskimo), who lived across Arctic North America before the ancestors of today's Inuit arrived. Igloolik, 4.8 x 10 x 8 cm, 2.5 x .9 x .6 cm, 32.5 x 8 x .6 cm. Eskimo Museum.

The hunter himself has made all of this equipment by hand from the materials offered in the Arctic, mostly parts of the animals he has hunted. He has spent hours making the harpoon head out of fragile bone or ivory, using tools made of bone, ivory, antler, rock, and sealskin. He has worked until the toggling harpoon head is perfectly shaped and morticed to fit snugly and securely on the tip of the harpoon shaft, as it must if it is to penetrate the tough hide of the seal. The combination of harpoon and harpoon head not only is cleverly designed but must be expertly manufactured: work a little bit more off here and there, round off this face a bit, taper this surface so that it will slide into the seal more easily.

⌒ LEAVING AT DAWN

The hunters would leave at the break of dawn, . . . they did not overnight—the hunters would be back that same day.

FRANK ANALOK, 82, CAMBRIDGE BAY, NUNAVUT

The hunters leave camp as a hint of daylight slowly spreads across the sky. Before departing, they might eat a piece of meat, if there is any left from the hunt the day before, or they might just drink some warmed seal blood or water. Then they head out across the ice. They walk, together with two or three dogs, to the chosen hunting area, sometimes 2 or 3 kilometers distant, where they have previously found some productive *agluit.*

As the hunters travel, they keep constant watch for changes in the weather. They rarely get caught in a severe storm, and when they do, they have seen it coming—in the appearance of the sky and the feel of the wind—far enough in advance to make preparations to wait out the storm in relative comfort, or at least in safety. If necessary, they will build an iglu; one vital piece of equipment the hunter never travels without is his broad, machetelike snow-knife. They also keep an eye out for changes in the color of the ice; every hunter learns as a boy that new, thin, unsafe sea ice is very dark, almost black. Although accidents involving people breaking through thin ice are alarmingly frequent in southern Canada, across the Arctic, where ice travel is far more common, such accidents are extremely rare.

After a long walk across the sea ice, the hunters are thirsty. Each hunter has filled a pouch made of the skin of a seal flipper with snow and carries it next to his skin under his caribou parka. His

FACING PAGE

A seal hunter's *unaaq* (harpoon) with a strong sealskin line attached to the *naulaq* (harpoon head), north Baffin Island, 1950s. Northwest Territories Archives (N-1991-059-0247). Photo by Doug Wilkinson.

OVERLEAF

On the sea ice off north Baffin Island, 1950s. Northwest Territories Archives (N-1991-059-0244). Photo by Doug Wilkinson.

body heat melts the snow, providing a ready supply of drinking water. The hunters do not eat snow, since it only increases one's thirst.

Knowing where to take the snow for meltwater at different times of the year is important. In this season, midwinter, the hunters collect snow to melt from the top layers of the generally flat snow cover on the sea ice, always being careful not to dig down near the surface of the salty sea ice. If there is an icy crust on top, they will take that, since it is denser than the snow beneath and is assuredly free of salt. Should they come across a snowdrift, where the wind has deposited an unusually high layer of snow, the granular snow found within the drift will have a higher water content than the fluffy wind-blown snow lying across the surface. In the spring, when the thaw begins, the sea ice freshens as the salt percolates downward, so ice taken from the top of an ice hummock will provide good fresh water even though it was originally frozen seawater. That good ice is easily identified by its color, which changes from the greenish turquoise hue of saltwater ice to a bluish white.

When the hunters finally arrive in the area where they know there must be seals, they go straight to work finding the *agluit* used by seals in the past few days. They use the shafts of their harpoons to poke the crust of snow that covers the sea ice, hoping to hit the tiny breathing holes underneath. It is worse than trying to find a needle in a haystack. They also look for visual clues; sometimes the snow over an *aglu* has a slight contour to it. It is very subtle, but a hunter can spot it on the flat sea ice from some distance away.

Often dogs aid hunters in their search. Even the hunters without enough dogs to pull a sled usually have one or two dogs to help find the *agluit*.

⌒ SEAL HUNTING WITH KAILEK

One time I went seal hunting with an old man named Kailek, the same elder who helped me make my *naulaq*. I was driving the snowmobile. He rode behind on my sled. But appearances notwithstanding, we both knew that he was taking me seal hunting. As we headed out onto the sea ice, he suggested we look for a crack in the ice because it would be easier to find the breathing holes there. We looked in vain but eventually found a patch of rough ice, where it must have been broken up before freezing solid. Just as in a crack, the ice cover here had been thinner when the seals were making their *agluit* in early winter. Kailek, like all Inuit men, knew this. We found a hole in the snow crust; it was less than 10 centimeters across, and beside it were signs of recent fox urine. Looking through the hole at the ice below, we could see a hole of open water at least twice that size. Open water: the seal had been up to breathe just recently; it was –30-something. The fox had left his mark, his "signpost" for future reference; some day he hoped to find a meal here. Meanwhile, his clue had led us to the hole. The snow cover was about 20 centimeters deep over that area of rough ice, so it was not easy to find the other breathing holes that must surely have been within easy walking distance. We looked, probing with our harpoon shafts, tips removed, but neither of us could find another *aglu*. "Dogs," said Kailek. "We need dogs." He explained that a good dog would sniff out the other holes in much the same way that the fox had found the one we saw.

∼ HUNTING WITH DOGS

In the old days, the hunters went with dogs, who helped to search for the agluit by smelling. With a heavier layer of snow, you could not see them, so it was the dogs who found them by smelling. I learned hunting, not from being taught in words. Sometimes when we were traveling by dogsled, the dogs would start going faster when they smelled an aglu. They could smell agluit, even along a flat surface, that would otherwise not be seen. They were a great help.

NOAH OQAITUK, 50, SANIKILUAQ, NUNAVUT
TRANSLATED BY QILUQQI

Noah Oquaituk

∼ DOGS CAN FIND SEALS' BREATHING HOLES

When seal hunting, you take along your dog, for clawing at seal holes. Some dogs have the knowledge to find seal holes and they quickly run to where there are seals. For some dogs it is hard to find seal holes. They are stubborn; without sniffing for seal holes, they just pass the hole as if it isn't there. Some Inuit dogs are like that and some dogs are smart— as soon as they get on ice, they start sniffing for holes. Because seal holes have strong smell, dogs can sense right away.

WILLIAM KUPTANA, BORN CIRCA 1915, SACHS HARBOUR, NORTHWEST TERRITORIES
TRANSLATED BY MARTHA ANGULALIK, COLLECTED BY ALLICE LEGAT

After a hunter has found an *aglu,* he usually peers through the hole to examine the water underneath. Black, open water is a sign that the seal has visited recently, probably within the last few minutes. Some hunters say they can even smell the residue of the seal's breath. Somewhat cloudy water, as it begins to freeze, suggests a longer time has passed since the seal's last visit. A thin crust of ice means even longer, and thick ice suggests an abandoned hole.

Each hunter sets up at a different hole. The hunter usually stands on something, such as an old piece of caribou hide with the hair still on, to muffle any sound his feet might make on the hard-packed, squeaky snow. One hunter has brought his son with him so that he can learn the traditional methods of the hunt. The boy walks in a wide circle around his father's *aglu.* As he walks, he slowly decreases the radius of the circle, hoping the noise of his feet on the ice will drive a seal in toward the breathing hole, where the hunter waits.

Ten men are scattered across the ice, bent over at the waist, motionless, waiting—tiny, insignificant figures in a vast panorama of whiteness. Each hunter is positioned on the downwind side of the hole so that the seal won't smell him when it surfaces, and the frigid wind blows in their faces. It is bone-chillingly cold, and there are no snowmobiles parked off to one side, no warm houses an hour's drive away, no refrigerators at home full of store-bought food, no stoves to turn on with the flick of a switch.

The hunters stand motionless for hours, harpoon in hand, waiting and concentrating, listening for the sound of the water rising up in a gushing sound. That means that the seal is swimming up toward the breathing hole. When the hunter hears a *whoosh,* the seal is exhaling and the hunter must strike downward with his harpoon.

Stone carving of a hunter standing over an *aglu* by Noah Koughajuke. Collection of The Winnipeg Art Gallery; Twomey Collection; with appreciation to the Province of Manitoba and Government of Canada.

⌒ WE COULD READ THE *AGLU*

*P*eople knew a lot in those days. When hunters located an aglu, they inspected it to find out how often a seal surfaced through it. If seals surfaced through a hole often, the area around the rim of the hole was full of clear pieces of ice. There was so much ice around some rims that your harpoon made noise when you dropped it. When seals didn't surface often, then the area around the rim looked soft, and even felt warm. You could also see small pieces of ice inside a hole where seals didn't surface often. Sometimes you could tell whether a seal will surface through the hole in the same day.

Markusi Ijaituk, born 1906, Ivujivik, Quebec, Avataq Cultural Institute

⌒ DETAILED KNOWLEDGE OF THE *AGLU*

FACING PAGE

**Carving of a hunter stand-
ing over an *aglu* with a seal
approaching from below.**

Courtesy Vic Pelletier.

*T*he aglu is where the seal will surface to take a breath through its nose.
If the hole is so small that it can breathe only through one side of its nose,
then it is called illuinaqqumituq *("single-sided"). A hunter who found*
such a hole would say "I found an illuinaqqumituq.*" It is such a tiny aglu*
to fit only one side of the nose. The two nostrils are unable to go out of this
hole. At the illuinaqqumituq, *in that tiny hole, it was very difficult to*
harpoon a seal because as soon as you moved, the seal would go away.
When you bring up your arm, your legs have moved, and the seal hears
the noise from there. Seals were often missed at this kind of aglu.

Others are called umirrumituq *("it will fit the whiskered part of the*
seal"). There are also agluit which are miqqutauralik *("it has little bits*
of fur around it"). And there are those called niaqqumituq *("the hole*
is large enough for the seal's head"). In spring, the miqqutauralik *has*
quite a bit of water; its edge has what looks like little hairs, which are
little formations of ice. These were words that a hunter would use when
they talked about the agluit that they found. They would say "I stood
over this kind of agluit." They talked about every little detail of the aglu.

JOHNNY MEEKO SR., BORN 1935, SANIKILUAQ, NUNAVUT, TRANSLATED BY QILUQQI

⌒ WHICH WAY WILL THE SEAL FACE?

*W*here there's water current, which way a seal will face when coming
up in an aglu depends on the currents. If there is no current, a seal could
face any way. But they always face the current, when there is one. We
hunted bearded seals only in areas with water currents, so it was prob-
ably easier to tell which way a bearded seal would face when surfacing.

JIMMY KONEAK, BORN 1901, KUUJJUAQ, QUEBEC, AVATAQ CULTURAL INSTITUTE

Hunting the Seal 53

Each hunter hopes for success. But far more important, they all understand, is their collective success. If just one of them catches a single seal, everyone in camp will have something to eat and every iglu will have some blubber for the lamp. If several men catch seals, they will feast. If one of them is fortunate enough to catch two in the day at the *aglu,* he will consider it a very good day. More than that, and it will likely be a day he will never forget.

Hours pass. Finally, one hunter hears the gushing sound of a seal pushing water ahead of it through the conical hole in the ice. He reacts quickly and precisely, thrusting his harpoon down forcefully into the *aglu* and into the seal as it rises to the surface. Once the harpoon head is lodged beneath the skin of the seal, it comes off the end of the shaft as the hunter pulls back his harpoon. As tension comes onto the sealskin line tied to the middle of the harpoon head, it rotates inside the seal and turns perpendicular to the open cut through which it entered. In this way, the harpoon head acts as a toggle under the animal's skin. The seal is now firmly attached to the end of a strong length of sealskin rope. With one hand, the hunter holds the seal on the end of his rope. With his other hand, he uses the shaft of his disarmed harpoon to open the hole so that the seal can be pulled up on top of the ice, where it is killed by a quick, sharp blow to the head.

The young boy accompanying the hunters does not catch a seal this time. But he knows that when he does catch one there will be a special relationship between him and the seal. In some parts of the Arctic, tradition dictated that the first time a boy caught a seal at an *aglu,* he had to remove his parka and lie down on the ice so that the other hunters could drag the dead seal over his bare back or chest, thereby forging the link between the hunter and the seal,

Lucassie Kattuk

a sacred bond that would serve for the rest of the hunter's life. As a result, other seals would not fear the young hunter in the future.

∽ TRADITION OF THE FIRST HUNT

I have heard what they used to do when a boy caught a seal for the first time. They pulled the seal over the chest of the person who caught the seal, as he was lying on the ice. He lay on his back, and sometimes he took his parka off so his skin was exposed. The seal was pulled across the boy's chest, still attached to the naulak. *Then he would give the seal to his* sanariarruk, *the one who had dressed him when he was born.*

LUCASSIE KATTUK, BORN 1928, SANIKILUAQ, NUNAVUT
TRANSLATED BY QILUQQI

∽ THE FIRST HUNT

It was brought home for everybody. Everybody was very proud of the person who caught the seal. And he was usually very happy. It seemed like he would never forget about his first catch for the rest of his life. That's all I know. Even myself, I was like that. When I caught my first of each different animal it was a really great experience. I was proud that my parents saw it and that others around heard about it, a hunter's first catch.

JOHNNY MEEKO SR., BORN 1935, SANIKILUAQ, NUNAVUT
TRANSLATED BY QILUQQI

OVERLEAF

Eating raw liver from a freshly caught seal, on the sea ice, western Canadian Arctic, ca. 1915. Diamond Jenness Collection, Canadian Museum of Civilization (50923).

After the seal is lying dead on the ice, the hunter splits open the belly at just the right spot to remove the liver and a small piece of blubber. All the other hunters from nearby *agluit* gather to share in the first taste of the seal. The man who caught the seal kneels and carefully slices the fat and the steaming liver and lays them on the white snow. The other hunters kneel to one side and watch in silence, as if paying homage. Then they all eat together. It is part of the ritual, even a mark of respect. Afterwards, the hunter closes up the seal again, using a long bone needle, so that the seal will not lose any precious blood or internal organs.

Back at the camp, the women and children are waiting patiently, with a quiet resignation for whatever may come. There may be fresh meat, or there may not. With luck, they will know by nightfall.

⌢ RETURNING FROM THE SEAL HUNT

When a hunter returned from seal hunting, if he returned empty-handed, that was just how it was. Even if there were a few hunters that went seal hunting, they might all return empty-handed. That is how it used to be. I experienced this as a child.

EKVANNA, 75, CAMBRIDGE BAY, NUNAVUT

The hunter who caught the seal drags it back to his iglu, another arduous walk, this time in failing light. People in camp are happy to see that there will be some meat to eat. The hunter's wife immediately gives the seal a drink of fresh water as a mark of respect, and then she completes the butcher's task. The meat is distributed throughout the camp according to custom, certain pieces going to certain people, depending on relationships.

Mabel Ekvanna Angutalik

Dragging a seal back to camp after a successful hunt at the *aglu*, western Canadian Arctic, ca. 1915.

Diamond Jenness Collection,

Canadian Museum of Civilization

(20283).

⌢ GIVING THE SEAL A DRINK

As a mark of respect, many Inuit groups had a tradition of giving the dead seal a "drink" of fresh water before the butchering began. How this was done varied. In the northwest corner of Hudson Bay, 77-year-old Mikitok remembers seeing and following this practice: "When we got the *nattiq* back to the iglu, never out where it was caught, we took some snow, dipped it in melted water, and put it in the seal's mouth." In the central Arctic, another respected elder, Analok, described it like this: "Before you cut up a seal, you would get some meltwater from your mouth and pour it into the seal's snout. First you melt fresh snow in your mouth, then you pour it in the seal's mouth." In both regions, the hunter's wife performed the ritual. Mikitok said his people gave the drink of water only to *nattiq*, never to *ugjuk*, the bearded seal. In Alaska, the ritual was followed for all marine mammals; Inupiat of northern Alaska had a special pot made of either wood or pottery to be used for this purpose. The people of northeast Russia, who also gave seals a drink, believed that the act involving meltwater would keep the sea-ice leads from freezing over, giving easier access to the seals. Some Inuit believed that a seal refreshed in this manner would be more likely to return again in the form of another seal for another drink. In all cases, the idea was to appease the seal's spirit. "That custom was passed on from generation to generation," said Analok, "so that the hunter would catch seals again in the near future, so that the seal would be renewed."

Mikitok

FACING PAGE

An Inuit woman in the western Canadian Arctic chewing on sealskin to prepare it for sewing, ca. 1915. Diamond Jenness Collection, Canadian Museum of Civilization (20213).

The much larger bearded seal, *ugjuk*, can also be caught at an *aglu*. If a bearded seal is caught, it is considered a communal catch. Although the hunter receives a choice cut, the meat becomes the property of his entire camp. The *ugjuk* is butchered by the men, together, out on the ice, before returning to camp. Ask any old Inuit hunter, and he could show you how, in his region, the bearded seal's meat was cut up and indicate which piece went to which person in camp. In many places, the custom is followed to this day.

⌒ UGJUK

Bearded seals used to be hunted also with harpoons. When the ugjuk [bearded seal] comes up for air through the breathing hole, if the breath appears to be soft, that means even if it pulls the line after you strike, it will not be as strong even when it starts jerking the line. It is said that you need not be intimidated to make your strike. On the other hand, there is another ugjuk that comes up for air, which will make the small opening on the conical shaped aglu to whistle when it breathes, and that means this particular animal is not friendly. It will pull hard and give strong jerks. This animal is very lively because of the way it breathes. These were the things that the elders wanted us to know about.

If the ugjuk breathes softly, that means this animal is not going to give as much fight when attached to the harpoon line. The one that gives a whistling sound is very lively and will give you a big tug in comparison to the one that has a soft breath. When you make your strike you should pull out your harpoon immediately when your line gets attached and grab hold of the line with your other hand below the hand that you have on your line. One must be alert in harpooning a bearded seal, sometimes when the line slacks it will sharply jerk. So they can get you off guard. Indeed ugjuit are dangerous.

My father once caught a bearded seal and two of his fingertips, that is the index and ring finger, were all bruised up just like a button. As it turned out his hands almost got tangled. He said that he had to keep his hand from being jammed at the opening of the aglu, at the tip of the conical ventilation. He was not able to grab hold of the line with the other hand. When someone noticed that he was tugging on a seal, they came over to assist him.

GEORGE KAPPIANAQ, BORN 1917, IGLOOLIK, NUNAVUT, TRANSLATED BY LOUIS TAPARDJUK
IGLOOLIK INULLARIIT ELDERS SOCIETY, IGLOOLIK RESEARCH CENTRE (IE327)

FACING PAGE

Ugjuk, a bearded seal, on the sea ice, Bathurst Inlet, western Canadian Arctic, ca. 1915. Diamond Jenness Collection, Canadian Museum of Civilization (38656).

After the seal has been butchered and distributed, everyone gathers together to eat, to share in the spoils of the day's hunt, however meager, however bountiful. Every woman receives a small portion of the seal fat, which she will work, pounding it with the rounded end of a musk-ox horn, to render the oil used for the *qulliq*, the oil lamp, which lights and warms her family's iglu.

In the warmth of the *qulliq*'s soft light, the day ends with the hunters sharing their experiences of the day. Their thoughts are never far from the hunt.

⌒ HEATING THE IGLU BY *QULLIQ*

We used our qulliit to cook, to melt snow for water, warmth, and light. Sometimes we had just one qulliq, and if there were two women living in the same iglu there were two qulliit, one for each woman. There was just one qulliq if there was just one woman living in the iglu. Iglus were quite warm if there was enough seal oil. If it was warm, nothing inside the iglu was frozen, that is if people had enough seal meat and fat. If there weren't enough food or fat in the village it was cold inside our iglus. To have enough warmth and light we needed seal fat to keep our qulliit burning.

SARAH QALINGO, BORN 1912, IVUJIVIK, QUEBEC, AVATAQ CULTURAL INSTITUTE (05-TO9/1)

In most parts of the Canadian Arctic, the skull of the seal was discarded on the ice near where the seal was caught so that the seal's spirit could return to its home. In Greenland, however, there was a proscription against throwing seal skulls into the sea. Instead they were piled together, separate from other seal bones, in a heap

just outside the hunter's dwelling. One explanation, offered to an 18th-century visitor to Greenland, was that this was done so "that the souls of the seals may not be enraged and scare their brethren from the coast." Much the same practice was observed by early English navigators in the eastern Canadian Arctic. In Alaska, a 19th-century ethnographic researcher tried to buy seal skulls, which Inupiat had collected, and was refused. Another researcher in Chukotka had a similar experience.

Whether the skull was returned to the sea or never thrown in the sea, care was taken everywhere not to fracture it. These rituals were followed out of respect for the dead seal's spirit.

Moses Koihok

⌒ SHARING THE SPOILS OF THE HUNT

When I was a child I used to visit around. I had caribou clothing, not what we are wearing today. I had a caribou parka. The front would get wet, going in and out of iglus. The front of my parka would freeze. I used to visit when I was younger, to the elders, whoever had an iglu. Iglus would be frosted too, sometimes, from having no oil for heat.

I was going to tell stories about the old ways of hunting seals, for the blubber. Seal hunters would spread out on the ice, and later they would gather and drum dance. Sometimes hunters would bring home a number of seals or only one. Some would pull two, three, or one seal. Then take their intestines out and their liver and eat it. If a hunter had caught a seal, he would tell the rest of the hunters to join him in eating the liver and fat. The hunter would tell his companions to feast on seal liver and fat if he had caught many seals. If a hunter caught seals, he would tell his companions to get pieces of meat to share. That was how it was, as I was

saying earlier, during the long dark nights, early morning twilight. When hunters had caught their seal and Inuit had gotten their share, there would be many people gathered together in the successful hunter's iglu. You shared the blubber and meat with other Inuit, every portion of the seal meat. Even the broth you gave to the elders.

Many hunters would catch a lot of seals and share with others: the intestines, ribs, everything of the seal, but the flippers and paws would be left for the hunter. When even just one seal was caught, you let a child fetch to each household. The person that was butchering the seal would ask a younger child, either a male or female, to fetch for his or her relatives—that was how it used to be. If I was told to fetch seal meat to my relatives, I would respond right away. The seal's heart was the smallest part. The seal's heart, although small, was a delicacy. You had to cut pieces of the seal's heart to share amongst others in camp, no matter how small it can be. The rich seal broth too, even a small portion, you had to share with everyone in your camp. That was how the Inuit had shared their meat. They shared in the old days.

MOSES KOIHOK, BORN 1921, BATHURST INLET, NUNAVUT
TRANSLATED BY TOMMY KILAODLUK, COLLECTED BY DOUG STERN

⌢ THE HUNTERS' RETURN

Upon their [the hunters'] return we would discover that no seal had been caught. After they had returned the men would get indoors and you could see that they are so passionately sorry. They are so sorry that they have not caught a seal this day and they feel so bad about it. Since there is hot water on the meager fire, the hunters will get a drink of hot water. Once we get to sleep we would seem to get warm.

The following day when we wake up we would see that the weather had improved dramatically so it is now a nice day. Again the hunters leave for their hunting ground. There is still a little bit of fuel to burn because of very careful management of the supply and by being frugal, as there is now only one qulliq that is allowed to burn despite the fact that the interior of the iglu is cold by then.

When the hunters return they would have caught numerous seals. The qulliit would be fueled so now the dwellings get warm. When the seal is cut up each household gets what they need from this seal and soon invitations are extended for cooked meat. When more than one seal is caught invitation will be announced for cooked meat in the morning before the hunters again go out to hunt. After the hunters had eaten they would again leave for their hunting grounds. We would be faced with hard and miserable times, but when seals are caught it once again becomes enjoyable and the dwelling again becomes warm. That was the way we lived.

RACHAEL UJARASUK, BORN 1914, IGLOOLIK, NUNAVUT, TRANSLATED BY LOUIS TAPARDJUK,
IGLOOLIK INULLARIIT ELDERS SOCIETY, IGLOOLIK RESEARCH CENTRE (IE012)

◡ OLD TABOOS AND CUSTOMS FOR SEALS

These are some of the old rules of the Iglulingmiut and Aivilingmiut, two groups of Inuit in Canada's central Arctic.

As long as a newly captured seal has not been cut up, the following things are taboo:

> *Rime must not be wiped from the ice window.*
> *Skins from the sleeping platform must not be shaken out over the floor.*
> *The mats of plaited willow twigs must not be straightened or rearranged.*
> *No oil must be spilled from the lamp.*
> *No work must be done with stone or wood.*
> *Women must not comb their hair, wash their faces or dry any footwear.*

When a bearded seal has been captured, no scraping of hair from skins must be done for three days.

When seals are caught, it is not allowed to shift camp the next day, but not until two days after the first catch; this is because the seals would be offended if the hunters were not grateful for the catch they got.

All bearded seals caught require a special sacrifice. The Mother of the Sea Animals is particularly fond of bearded seals, and they know it, and when they have been killed by human hands, they go to her and complain; therefore special precautions are observed when a bearded seal has been killed.

If a seal is brought into an iglu and there is a widow of not more than a year's standing present, she must at once pull up her hood, and she may not express her pleasure at the capture.

Young girls present in a house where a seal is being cut up must take off their boots and remain barefooted as long as the work is in progress.

When a seal has been cut up and lies in pieces on the floor, a lump of fresh snow is laid on the spot where its head was, and trodden down there. The Sea Spirit does not like women to tread on the spot where the seal's head has lain.

As long as a ringed seal remains on the floor and has not yet been cut up, the sleeping rugs must not be arranged, set in place or shaken.

The soul of a seal resides in the naulaq *(harpoon head) for one night after the seal has been killed. Hence the harpoon head, with line and shaft, must be taken into the iglu and placed beside the* qulliq *(lamp) when the hunter comes home after killing a seal. This is done in order that the soul may be warm throughout the night it remains in the* naulaq *which killed the seal.*

Women must never make sinews [to use as thread for sewing] of a ringed seal. Anyone trying to sew with sinews of a ringed seal will die of it, for the sinews of the seal are so short that the animal is ashamed of them, and its soul will kill anyone trying to use them.

COLLECTED BY KNUD RASMUSSEN, 1922

⌒ SHARING THE MEAT

When hunters caught a seal at the floe edge in winter, they ate the flesh around the tail and the liver on the spot. They divided the rest of the seal for the people. Even the fat was divided. Although a single seal was caught, if there were a lot of people, the hunter who caught a seal would even cut the ribs to pieces so that everyone could get a share. If the Inuit knew there were some people in another camp who needed food, they brought some of their catch to them. I remember a time when the Inuit were so helpful toward each other.

A single tiny seal would seem to grow so much bigger when generously shared. Pieces of meat were taken to everyone. The back part and the tail were mostly eaten by men, although they could be eaten by anyone. Men ate mostly fleshy parts. Women ate bony parts like the part just above the flipper. Pieces of bones with little meat on them were thought to be for women. Women would rather eat meat around the bones than pieces of meat without bones. Although there was no set rule, those were the preferences of men and women.

MITIAJUK ATTASI NAPPALUK, BORN 1931, KANGIRSUJUAQ, QUEBEC,
AVATAQ CULTURAL INSTITUTE

FACING PAGE

While basking on the ice in spring, a seal often looks up warily to check for danger. *Untitled (seal)*, prior to 1971. Ottochie Ashoona, Cape Dorset, 1942–1970. Stone, 12.6 x 21.6 x 7.6 cm.

Collection of The Winnipeg Art Gallery; Twomey Collection; with appreciation to the Province of Manitoba and Government of Canada (1103.71). Photo by Ernet Mayer, The Winnipeg Art Gallery.

The Spring Hunt

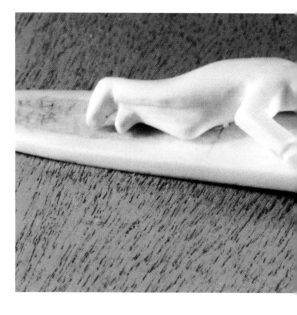

*I was very careful in trying to
catch my first seal. I worked hard
for it. I wanted it. I did not want
to lose to the other young people.
I was trying hard too. I was
doing it the way they used to
hunt for seals, by imitating the
noises of seals. That is how I
caught it, while it was basking,
very close by.*

Davidee Eyaituk, born 1935,
Sanikiluaq, Nunavut
translated by Qiluqqi

Spring has arrived in the Arctic.
Both *nattiq* and *ugjuk* are lying on
the ice napping, or "basking," as Inuit say. Some seals sleep for only
ten to twenty seconds at a time, between raising their heads for a
look around. More commonly, they will nap for a minute or more
between checks. On warm days, they sleep more soundly, however
briefly.

Mikitok decides to show me one of the traditional hunting
methods that Inuit use in spring. He lies on the surface of the sea
ice on his right side, his right elbow, forearm, hip, and leg all in
contact with the ice. His upper right arm supporting his upper
body is perfectly vertical, and his forearm lies flat on the ice,
aligned exactly with the direction of the seal. His body must be
precisely positioned. About 300 meters away, a seal is sleeping in

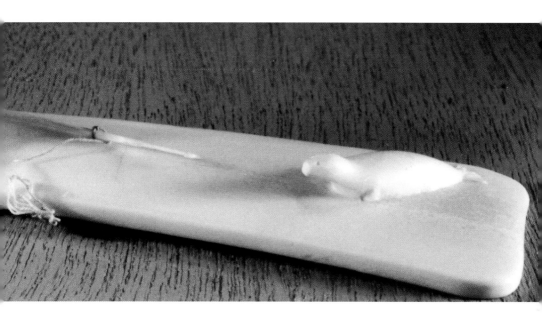

the sun. When the seal raises its head and sees Mikitok, he tucks his right arm under his body, hiding his hand under his hip, and lies down on the full length of his right side so that he looks like a seal. His right leg is tucked under and behind his left leg. He then uses the foot of his left leg to scratch the ice. When the seal hears the scratching, it relaxes and puts its head down.

Mikitok now lifts his head up, supports himself on his right elbow, and slowly moves a meter or two toward the seal. When the seal looks up again, Mikitok puts his head down and scratches the ice with his heel. This time the seal does not seem reassured, so Mikitok makes a seal-like noise with his mouth. He wants the seal to look at him so that it can decide that he is not a threat.

Man Stalking a Seal on the Ice, **Repulse Bay, 1948. Mark Tungilik, 1913–1986. Ivory, 1.3 x 15.3 x 3.8 cm.**

Eskimo Museum. Reprinted by permission of the Inuit Art Foundation.

～ MY FATHER TAUGHT ME
TO HUNT BY *AURIAQ*

My father use to stalk seals by auriaq [also aurnaq, *meaning to stalk them by crawling motion until they were very close*]. Sometimes he would get really close to them. I tried once using this technique as I used to watch him often doing it, but the seal dove on me . . .

Apparently, the one that dove on me using this technique (this was told to me by my father after I got back; he had been watching me on the telescope) was due to the fact I was curled too much, my shoulders were stooped too low, while my buttocks were flush to the ground. The proper way was to get the seal's attention. When it looked at you, you should put your arm to your side straight down while you lie on your side so that the width of your upper body becomes wider. One also should not face the seal in line but turn sideways whenever the seal looks up; when you start to crawl again towards it you may head straight for it. One must take time to stalk a seal using this technique. One must always be gradual in approaching a seal in this manner; only then can one get to it.

My father used to grab a seal before it dove through the breathing hole. When he got so close to a basking seal using this technique, he would put his hands out in a manner that he would grab the seal's hind flippers, the hind flippers would start to curl. All along the seal would be facing the other direction. He used to tell me that when one started to go for the hind flipper easily it is difficult to grab one as it will curl away, so one must grab it with a jab.

MARK IJJANGIAQ, BORN 1923, IGLOOLIK, NUNAVUT, TRANSLATED BY LOUIS TAPARDJUK
IGLOOLIK INULLARIIT ELDERS SOCIETY, IGLOOLIK RESEARCH CENTRE (IE086)

⁓ HOW I LEARNED TO *AURNAQ*

At *Duke of York Bay, just when Louis and Leonie were born, my grand-father and I went to camp near the point. There were lots of seals near our camp. So I took my harpoon and went down toward the seals. With my harpoon I could catch a seal, without shooting it. So I went toward the seals and my grandfather stayed at the camp. I tried to harpoon two seals, but I missed. I went back up to camp. When I approached my grandfather, he was singing Ai-ya-ya—it seemed like he was just singing, not thinking of anything. He had made some tea and boiled seal. After I had some tea, I told him about the seals I had tried to harpoon but had kept missing. My grandfather said, "Of course you lost those two seals. You did it the wrong way. Let's go down to the ice."*

So we went outside and down to the ice to a flat area. He lay down on the flat surface. "You do it this way. You're doing it wrong," he said. He showed me how. "I do it this way," he said, lying down flatter on the ice. He made me understand how to do it properly. I got pretty embarrassed. . . .

We slept for a while in our tent. After I woke up, I saw a few seals, but I didn't bother to go catch them, because I was embarrassed in front of my grandfather. He's just going to keep watching me and tell me what to do again, I thought. So, without catching any more seals, we went back to our main camp.

Later, I went down to the ice alone. It seemed like the seals were so easy. I could catch them easily. I could do anything, because my grand-father taught me a lesson. Not too long after that, my grandfather died. So I regretted that I didn't let him watch me again, because I was too embarrassed. I was upset at myself. If I had let him watch me one more time, I would have at least known a bit more. But I lost that. I thought my grandfather knew everything about how to hunt.

MIKITOK, 77, CORAL HARBOUR, NUNAVUT

Mikitok moves very slowly. As the seal gets used to his presence, he can move a bit more quickly. When he is quite close, he bangs the ice with his hand so that the seal—now confident that it is in the presence of another seal—gets used to a different noise. When Mikitok has crawled close enough, he leaps to his feet and harpoons the unsuspecting seal.

While asleep, according to Mikitok, a seal does not breathe, sometimes for several minutes. When it opens its eyes, it breathes at the same time. Mikitok has observed this phenomenon when he hunts; he has seen a seal's flank move just as the seal's eyes open. This is especially useful as a way to know that the seal is now looking at you, for sometimes the seal does not raise its head. So Mikitok watches for the light reflecting off the seal's dark skin as it breathes and takes his cue. "It's like I am talking to the seal, saying 'Look up' or 'Lie down.' If you do it correctly, it's like you control the seal."

When he was younger, without a high-powered rifle, or when bullets were in short supply, Mikitok relied on this method of hunting to catch the seals needed for his family's camp on the north shore of Southampton Island. He has not forgotten how to "communicate with the seals."

This method of hunting, called *aurnaq*, is one of several methods Inuit traditionally used in spring, usually in June, when the seals are molting. Earlier in the spring, other methods were used.

In April, when most of the waters inhabited by ringed seals are still solidly frozen to a depth of at least a meter, most often more, the females climb out of the water through one of the breathing holes that they have kept open all winter long. It is time to give birth. Each seal chooses a hole where the wind-blown snow has built up above the ice surface, as it naturally does around obstructions such as ice hummocks and pressure ridges, or sometimes over an old tidal crack in the ice. In the resulting accumulated snow, the pregnant seal hollows out a lair 2 or 3 meters across and gives birth to a single pup. Most ringed seals around the circumpolar world give birth this way, but in the relatively temperate Sea of Okhotsk, east of Russia and north of Japan, ringed seals whelp out in the open on pack ice, much as more southern seals such as harps and hoods do.

Either way, only the mother cares for the newborn, nursing the pup until nearly the end of May, by which time it has doubled its weight. During that time, the pup starts to become comfortable in the water. The mother seal constructs a second, smaller lair above another hole, to which the pup swims unaccompanied by its mother. During this initial phase of its life, the pup is strongly bonded to its mother, and the mother is protective of her pup and will attempt to defend it against predation by a polar bear or an Arctic fox.

Inuit hunters have used their knowledge of this bond to entrap the mother seal. First, the hunter catches the pup by jumping on top of the lair to break open the snow crust and then grabbing the surprised pup. If the mother is in the lair, she is usually quick enough to escape down the hole. To lure the mother back, the hunter then dangles the pup on the end of a sealskin rope in the water of the seal's breathing hole. Seeing her pup in the water, the mother grasps it with her flippers and swims up to the surface to return it to the ice. At that moment the hunter strikes with his harpoon.

⌒ MAKING AN *AVATAQ*

From the skin of a seal, the hunter would start making floats
before it was late in the spring. He would first have to catch
a seal that he would use the skin to make a float with; he
had to be very careful that there was minimal wound
holes to the animal when he stalks the seal by auriaq.
This was done before the seals start to molt in the
spring. When skins from seals which had started to
molt were used, the air tended to leak when the float
was inflated, even when there are no holes in the
skin. When the seals are molting, the membrane
changes as new fur on the skin starts to grow.

When they find that the skin leaks air they would
pour oil into the skin, and the oil would seep into the
skin, so the float would stay inflated longer without
any leaks. The best oil is from bearded seal blubber,
where you would cook the blubber to render the oil,
which could be used for many purposes.

Floats were very important implements as they
played a very important role in securing food and
other necessities at the time when we only depended on
harpoons to catch marine animals.

Noah Piugaattuk, born 1900, Igloolik, Nunavut
translated by Louis Tapardjuk,
Igloolik Inullariit Elders Society,
Igloolik Research Centre (ie136)

Untitled (Hunter with Sealskin Float), 1957.
Isah Ajagutaina Tukala,
Puvirnituq, 1905–1977.
Stone, antler, hide,
16.5 x 8.9 x 20.0 cm.
Collection of The Winnipeg Art Gallery;
the Swinton Collection; gift of the
Women's Committee (G-60-159).
Photo by Ernest Mayer, The Winnipeg
Art Gallery.

OVERLEAF

A hunter surprising the
seals inside a birthing lair,
above an *aglu*, to catch the
newborn seal, north Baffin
Island, 1950s. Northwest
Territories Archives (N-1979-051-0686).
Photo by Doug Wilkinson.

⁓ SEALS WERE ESSENTIAL
TO OUR SURVIVAL

In the springtime, it was seal more than any other animal that was wanted, to get their blubber as a winter supply. In those days we didn't have Coleman stoves and so on. The oil lamp was the only source of heat and light. From what I remember, it was especially the seals' blubber that was especially wanted. Although they wanted the other animals too, it was especially the ringed seal blubber, and the bearded seal too, that was wanted. We wanted the other animals which had oil too, but it seemed like it was the ringed seal which was most available, although not all the time either. Above all else, they were the most important.

The seals have been the most important to the Inuit. As Arctic people we have used seals for our survival.

PAULOOSIE EKIDLAK, BORN 1934, SANIKILUAQ, NUNAVUT
TRANSLATED BY QILUQQI

⁓ HUNTING IN APRIL

When daylight became longer, hunters would harpoon so many seals at the seal holes. At times a hunter would harpoon and come home with four seals in one day when the weather wasn't too cold, around the month of April. Hunters would have no hard time catching seals when darkness was less and the coldest months were passed. The hunter would return home with three or four seals that same day. Sometimes hunters would catch more seals if they found the right spot where seals were.

WILLIAM KUPTANA, BORN CIRCA 1915, SACHS HARBOUR, NORTHWEST TERRITORIES
TRANSLATED BY MARTHA ANGULALIK, COLLECTED BY ALICE LEGAT

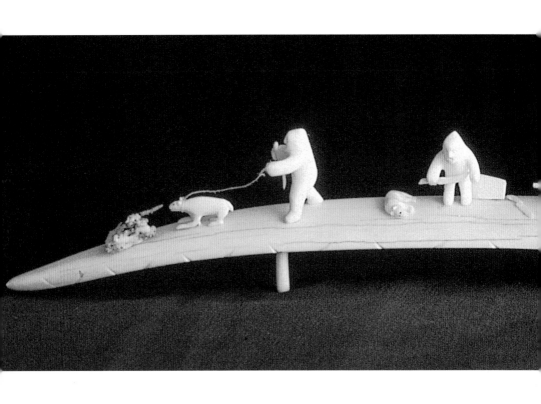

Spring Hunting at the
Aglu, Pelly Bay, 1949.
Antonin Attark, 1909–1960.
Ivory, 17.4 x 48.2 x 5.3 cm.

∿ FINDING A SEAL LAIR

As we started to hunt for seal pups we were told that when we came across seal breathing holes where there was a large buildup of snowdrift, we should open the breathing holes so that they are exposed, as there might be a seal pup in the den, especially on the lee side of pressure ridges where the snow banks had built up. When we walk towards the sun it is easier to determine that the snow is slightly sunk, which is an indicating factor that there is hollow under it, which suggests a den. This is easily identifiable as the sunken surface is different from other surroundings. There are some traces of frost on the surface. At this time the hunters would run to the location and jump on it to break through the den.

ZACHARIAS AQQIARUQ, BORN 1926, IGLOOLIK, NUNAVUT
TRANSLATED BY LOUIS TAPARDJUK, IGLOOLIK INULLARIIT ELDERS SOCIETY,
IGLOOLIK RESEARCH CENTRE (IE122)

At the same time that mother and pup are sheltered in their lair, somewhere nearby there is probably a male in his own, slightly smaller lair. Inuit call the males *tiggak,* referring to the strong odor of the bull seals in rut. A few weeks after a female has given birth, she mates again. Implantation is delayed, however, and the new fetus does not begin development for about three months. Meanwhile, her current pup will become entirely independent by the time the ice breaks up in July.

Bearded seal pups are born on the ice from late April to early May and stay with their mothers only about two weeks before becoming independent. Like their smaller cousins, these females then immediately mate, but implantation is delayed until mid-summer. It is during mating that the bearded seals exhibit one of their most curious characteristics, whistling in a way that one observer likened to the sound of a plane dropping a bomb in an old World War II movie. The sounds are so audible, transmitted underwater, that during open-water hunting by kayak, Inuit used to listen for the bearded seal by putting an ear to the handle of a paddle with its blade in the water.

In June, the sea ice in much of the Arctic—as seen from the air—is littered with tiny black specks: seals basking in the spring sun. They are molting, and perhaps the sun's warmth makes them feel better or raises their skin temperature enough to help the new hair grow back. This is a favorite time among Inuit for hunting seals and is traditionally when they have hunted most by *aurnaq.*

Whatever method of hunting was used in the spring, most rituals of respect and customs of sharing remained the same as for a seal caught through the ice during the long winter months. The seal would be given a drink of water before it was butchered, and pieces of meat would be distributed throughout the camp.

FACING PAGE

North Baffin Island, 1950s.

Northwest Territories Archives

(N-1991-059-0232). Photo by Doug

Wilkinson.

～ NOTHING WAS WASTED

There was nothing wasted. If it was a male adult bearded seal, it was used as a kayak skin, or it was marinated [to eat, as a delicacy], or they would scrape the fur off to make boot soles or ropes. It was very useful. We used the muscles of the bearded seal's flipper bones for sinew. Ringed seal skin was scraped in the summer to make clothing, and things like mitts, inner boots. It has many uses too.

ANNIE EETOOK, BORN 1930, KANGIRSUK, QUEBEC,
AVATAQ CULTURAL INSTITUTE

～ DANCE TO THE WHISTLING OF A BEARDED SEAL

You would probably dance to the whistling of a bearded seal if you should hear it. It's a call they make for other bearded seals. When we heard that sound, we'd stop our kayaks, lift our paddles, and listen using our paddles. We would then estimate the location of the seal and head in that direction. I was taught how to find one, so when I heard it, I'd try to go straight to it. When my brothers and I heard a seal, we'd part and each search for the seal that made the noise. It wasn't always easy to find. It floated as it called. Inuit don't hunt using that method nowadays. Inuit hunters were very brave then. A bearded seal has emerged under my kayak twice. You have to be careful!

JIMMY KONEAK, BORN 1901, KUUJJUAQ, QUEBEC,
AVATAQ CULTURAL INSTITUTE

The Winter and Summer Hunts in Greenland

Without seals, this place could not have survived.
We stayed here because of the seals and the narwhals.

MARTIN ANGUBESEN, 57, KITSISSUARSUIT, GREENLAND

THE HUNTERS have set out early in the morning on this winter day. They are dressed in sealskin clothing, and they are traveling by dogsled. As they travel, they examine the sky: the dark water is reflected on the clouds above, providing a map of where to find the open water and the seals.

When the hunters arrive at the floe edge bordering on open water, they find positions on the edge of the ice. Each hunter partially obscures himself with a homemade blind or a piece of ice, his kayak at the ready beside him, and waits for a seal to rise.

At last a seal surfaces near one of the hunters. He throws his harpoon, hitting the seal with enough force that the sharp tip easily penetrates the seal's tough hide. The *naulaq* at the harpoon tip is connected by a long sealskin line to an *avataq* (a sealskin float); after the hunter harpoons his quarry, he quickly launches his kayak to recover the float and pull in the wounded seal.

This is how hunters have traditionally hunted in Kitsissuarsuit, a tiny island off the west coast of Greenland, roughly a kilometer across. It lies 20 kilometers offshore, alone at sea in Greenland's vast Disko Bay. Its only companions out there are the icebergs, lots of them; for centuries, they were the major freshwater delivery system.

The hills on this picturesque green island rise to 43 meters above sea level. Its shoreline includes several little coves and one well-protected natural harbor. Surrounding the harbor is a quiet village, the brightly colored houses scattered up the hillsides, looking down on the little harbor or out to sea. Although the houses seem to have been built at random, each is positioned to take maximum advantage of its view.

This is a community of hunters, who constantly watch the sea. A well-worn track, trod by generations of villagers, runs up the hillside from the harbor and then splits off to climb each of the hills toward the scattered houses. The pattern draws you in, and you immediately want to stay. It is no different for the 120 people who live here. The people of Kitsissuarsuit are content with their lives on the tiny island. It is the hunting ground they know best. Young men who learn to hunt here, while they may go away to school or work for a few years, typically come home to Kitsissuarsuit when they marry, to settle down to the hunting lifestyle they know best. Few men from elsewhere move here. The women who come here are brought in as newlyweds. It is an unusually traditional hunting community, with a remarkably stable population.

⌒ I WAS BORN HERE

I *was born here, I've lived here all my life, and I hope I'll stay here till the end. Normally, if you are born here, you are very attached to it.*

JOHANNES JEREMIASSEN, 50, KITSISSUARSUIT, GREENLAND

It takes only five minutes to ascend a path to the crest of a hill in the center of the island. Someone is usually posted on the weathered wooden bench that sits there, looking out to sea with binoculars, checking the weather and watching for seals and whales—

though no formal rotation of the duty exists. Sea mammals are the mainstay of the diet of the people in Kitsissuarsuit, and they live today by hunting, as they always have. They hunt ringed seals, beluga, and narwhal throughout the winter at the ice edge, and occasional fin whales in late summer and fall in open water. In summer and fall they mainly hunt harp seals in open water.

The annual migration of the harp seals hunted on Greenland's west coast—one of the three populations of harp seals in the world—is a remarkable phenomenon, 4000 kilometers of precise navigation. From the ice pack off Newfoundland, where the seals give birth, mate, and molt within the space of a few weeks, most of the seals head north up the coast of Labrador in early June. The newborn pups, having doubled their weight in the first two weeks of life, are left behind. At the bottom of Baffin Island, the population splits: the younger seals, up to three years old, head across to Greenland and spread along the west coast all the way to the northern tip. The older harps either do not make the crossing or they return as the season advances; they tend to summer in Canadian waters, heading north to Lancaster Sound or in through Hudson Strait to Foxe Basin and as far west as Igloolik.

All of the harp seals in this northwestern Atlantic population spend their summer feeding in Arctic waters and then start their southward migration in late September, when freeze-up begins. Unlike ringed and bearded seals, the harp seals are not able to survive under the ice. By late February, they are congregating once again on the ice off Newfoundland or in the Gulf of St. Lawrence, and the cycle starts over.

There are various scientific theories about how the seals find their way on this long migration. Perhaps they can differentiate between the coastal waters of Labrador and the deeper offshore

OVERLEAF

Inuit in Greenland butchering the seal after a successful hunt, 1909.
Arnold Heims Collection, © Arktisk

Institut (30456)

water by color, or perhaps they use changes in water temperature or in winds and currents to navigate. To Inuit who have always hunted the seals, however, there is no real mystery about their ability to travel great distances. Many animals in their domain—like the caribou and the geese—accomplish much the same feat. And Inuit themselves have always traveled great distances over land and water, without maps, but with an intimate knowledge of where they were going. The suggestion that the seals simply have an innate sense of navigation is supported by the fact that the newborn pups, only a few months old, travel north for the first time independently, unaccompanied by the older seals, who have gone well ahead.

Meanwhile, the other two populations of harp seals are following similar patterns elsewhere in the Arctic. Traditionally, Sami people in northern Norway and Finland and along the coast of the Kola Peninsula harvested these seals for both their skins and their meat. Certainly in the 19th century, and probably before that, Russian sealers from the *kolkhozes* (fishing villages) along the coast of northwest Russia walked far out onto the ice fields of the White Sea. In 1910 ice-breaking ships came into use to help the hunters reach the whelping patch.

Nowhere, however, is the indigenous tradition of hunting harp seals stronger than in Greenland. Nowhere in the circumpolar world have these seals been more important to the people. Today the annual harvest in Greenland is about 70,000 harps, the vast majority of which are caught along the west coast.

⌁ THE IMPORTANCE OF THE RINGED SEAL

Harp seals, while always important, have not always been the most hunted at Kitsissuarsuit. Hans Hansen, 78, says that his grandfather—who was born in the 1840s and also lived on this tiny island—caught about 500 ringed seals in an average year and somewhat fewer harp seals, hunting with a harpoon from his kayak. "In those days, sometimes the water was black with ringed seals, he used to say," Hansen recalls.

Hansen himself remembers when there were many more ringed seals around Kitsissuarsuit even in summer. Elsewhere in Greenland, in the far north and along the east coast, the harp seal is still surpassed in abundance and importance by the ringed seal. Ask Inuit there, or throughout Canada's Arctic, which of the seals has always been most important to their people, and there is little question what the answer will be: unanimously, they will give top honors to the ringed seal, *nattiq*.

⌁ HARP SEALS

We even preferred the big harp seals because they had lots of meat. We didn't really think about the taste then, only about how much meat it had, and the skin for clothing.

The adult harp seals used to stay around here longer in early winter, congregating in areas of open water. There were no "noisemakers" [commercial fishing boats and big cargo ships] back then. My father hunted seals from his kayak with just a harpoon. My generation has always used a rifle.

MARTIN ANGUBESEN, 57, KITSISSUARSUIT, GREENLAND

Many men in the village can relate tales of hunting by kayak, which remained commonplace until the 1980s. Jakob Angubesen, for example, now 64, built his first kayak at age 15 and remembers hunting from it in the open water of summer and in the frozen winter, when he carried the kayak out to the floe edge to hunt for whales and ringed seals. Unlike most of the Canadian Arctic, and the far north Thule district of Greenland, the hunters here never have to stand over a seal's breathing hole, waiting, even in winter, because there is always open water no more than a few hours away by dogsled, and the ringed seals tend to congregate along the ice edge. Today most people use dog teams and sledges to transport themselves and their boats out to the floe edge—snowmobiles are banned from the island and its surroundings because the hunters fear the noise will disturb the wildlife on which they still depend.

Jakob Angubesen

In the open-water season (summer and fall), hunters paddled out to sea in search of seals. To stay dry, they wore complete suits of sealskin clothing, neck and sleeves fitting tightly enough to prevent any water from entering. In stormy conditions, quite prevalent in Greenland's coastal waters, they needed to be adept at turning their kayak upside down and then righting it again (what kayakers now call an Eskimo roll) in anticipation of a large crashing wave, which might otherwise break their backs. This technique worked with the Greenlandic style of kayak but not, for example, with the bigger and flatter kayaks of north Baffin Island. Greenlandic hunters used to say that it was easier to sneak up on the seals in really stormy conditions, when they could use the waves to conceal their approach. But it was a very dangerous enterprise. Once close enough, the hunter thrust his harpoon into the seal.

Although the technology has changed, the cycle of life in Kitsissuarsuit is much the same now as it has been for generations.

Nᵒ 2.   Torúkamiuk sanarfivâ

Ātāmik pimartoḳe ínardlungmut nauligpoḳ.

Hunting by kayak as
depicted by the
Greenlandic artist Aron.

Greenland National Museum.

It is one of the more traditional Inuit villages left in the circumpolar world, more dependent than most on the bounty of the sea for its survival. Most communities have been pulled more completely into the modern era of wage employment.

⌁ THE SUMMER MIGRATION

The older people on the island remember when it was customary to leave during the summer, when it was difficult to obtain enough food from the hunt. Dorothe Angubesen, born on the island in 1914, recalled the annual summer trip by sealskin *umiaq* (plural: *umiat*) from the island into the depths of Disko Bay, where people went to harvest capelin. At that time, according to community records, the population of Kitsissuarsuit was 166, of whom 57 were 12 years old. There were 53 hunters, 60 sealskin kayaks, 9 sealskin *umiat*, 3 wooden boats, 8 dog sledges, 63 rifles, and 95 seal nets (for use under the ice). They lived in 17 houses and 10 sealskin tents. For the annual summer migration, as many as 20 people rode in each *umiaq*, mostly women and children, the women paddling, with one man to steer. Other men traveled alongside in their sealskin kayaks. This snapshot of life in west Greenland comes from the first half of the 20th century, not that long ago.

⌒ A TRUE STORY OF A SEAL HUNT
DURING DIFFICULT TIMES

My father and I would walk to the floe edge when the currents were right so that if my father caught a seal the seal could be carried to the edge. My older brother and I went to the bottom of the bight at the open water. Sometimes the water was calm so that seals could be seen, but they were not able to catch any seals. As it turned out there was something among us that made it extremely difficult for us to catch any game. We would see seals bobbing their heads in the water some distance from the edge. No one was able to catch any seals. The weaker dogs soon started to dwindle in numbers due to starvation.

We were not being successful in this place, so we moved on to the ice near Uglirjjuaq where there was a floe edge below Igjuriktuq. We settled on the ice when we passed Uglirjjuaq to the floe edge, where there is a constant open water when the tide is going out and with the wind. No one had caught a seal to this date. We were left with seven dogs, which were the only ones left from the team. My father's dog team had some left as well. The ones that were left were the lead dogs in the team as they were fed a small amount of food.

The wind was blowing, but it was not strong. The snow was not drifting all that much. My older brother was asked to go to the trading post to get something that we could use for food. He might have asked him to get some on credit, but there were few fox pelts. At the same time me and my father went down to the floe edge. As we camped on the ice, the floe edge was not that far so that we could get to it without any difficulty. We were on the land-fast ice.

My older brother left in the morning, while we left at dawn when we could see with the light, that is with my father. He and I would walk, at least I would do most of the walking and sometimes my father would also start to walk then get on the sled for a ride. The dogs were still able to carry the load, though in weakened state. He and I spent time at the floe edge, but we could not see any seals even when the wind was not strong. Soon the night started to fall upon us. Naujan was not far from where we were, but it was not all that close. We were on the sea ice of Naujan, between Uglirjjuaq and Tajarnniq, closer to Uglirjjuaq.

As the sun was just going down a seal finally surfaced, my father got the seal, which of course floated, so he went to get it. When he beached [pulled the boat back up on the ice] the sun had disappeared out in the horizon. He slit the seal open and cut a piece of blubber, and then removed the under belly of the seal, and I believe that he butchered the seal. He then put out some blubber so that it could harden. Then he fed me a little piece so that I would not get too thirsty. He advised me that I should not eat too much in its fresh state. I ate a little piece of meat and liver so that I got much warmer then we proceeded to go home. My father would walk alongside the sled as we slowly headed for home. I too would walk a little bit, but I soon would get on the sled for the ride. He sometimes asked me to walk.

When we finally got home my mother pounded blubber which fueled her qulliq and lit her qulliq. We got into the dwelling. My mother proceeded to cook some meat. It was a joyous and warm occasion. I believe we had gone to sleep, or at least had gone to bed when we heard my older brother arrive. He brought something to eat that was given to him for free by the Hudson's Bay Company which consisted of flour, and biscuit, according to the rules of the police. We now had food to eat after two months without ever seeing food to eat.

GEORGE KAPPIANAQ, BORN 1917, IGLOOLIK, NUNAVUT, TRANSLATED BY LOUIS TAPARDJUK
IGLOOLIK INULLARIIT ELDERS SOCIETY, IGLOOLIK RESEARCH CENTRE (IE330)

A Sacred Link

A long time ago, the people were happy and it seemed they had nothing to worry about even though they had no material things.

Ekvanna, 75, Cambridge Bay, Nunavut

For Inuit, traditionally, hunting was the basis of survival; theirs is a hunting culture. But the Inuit hunt is different from the typical western hunt, in which a more powerful, technically better equipped, or perhaps smarter being tracks down and kills an inferior being. The difference may lie in the notion of "soul." Whereas the European world-view is that only humans have a soul, the traditional Inuit belief is that all beings have a soul. For Inuit, success at the hunt was a result of respecting the soul of their quarry, of holding the proper attitude toward the seal.

Traditionally, the hunt is the pact between Inuit and the seal. The Inuit hunter is not extracting from the environment but creating a bond between his people and their environment. When the seal gives itself to the hunter, it is an act of sharing in which the seal is transformed from animal to human. Being consumed is a form of rebirth or renewal for the seal.

According to ancient Inuit philosophy, sharing among all beings makes survival in the Arctic possible. A real Inuk would never brag about his hunt, overhunt, or *not* hunt. Nor would he decline to share the hunt's reward, for to do so would be to contravene the basic laws of respect among all creatures, who exist as equals. To be disrespectful in this way would offend the seals and encourage them to disappear. And for Inuit through the centuries, life depended on the seals and on this pervasive respect for them.

A Pact for Survival

I think the seals have most helped the Inuit arrive to today.

JIMMY IQALUK, 52, SANIKILUAQ, NUNAVUT

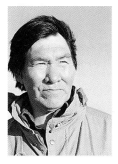

Jimmy Iqaluk

The New Economy

TODAY INUIT in Canada live in communities scattered across the North, in houses that are as modern, well-insulated, well-equipped, and comfortable as houses anywhere. The communities range from about three hundred to almost four thousand people. There are no roads connecting them to each other or to southern Canada. Every village has at least one store where a modest range of manufactured goods and imported foods are sold for three or four times what one would pay in southern Canadian cities. This high cost of living encourages most people to continue, to some degree, to depend on seals as a source of food.

In the past, Inuit used every part of the seal—the meat for food, sealskin for clothing and other supplies, and the blubber for fuel for heat and light. Inuit continue to eat seal meat as at least part of their diet, but they no longer wear as much sealskin clothing or use blubber for fuel. Instead, they need money to buy manufactured clothing and fuel. Moreover, although the new technology—snowmobiles and rifles—has allowed them to maintain the traditional hunt, they now must travel greater distances to hunt and hunting is more difficult, more time-consuming, more dangerous, and more expensive than in the past.

FACING PAGE

Father and child in sealskin kayak, northern Quebec, ca. 1920. Notman Photographic Archives, McCord Museum of Canadian History, Montreal (MP-1976.25.135).

OVERLEAF

Inuit women in Greenland preparing sealskins in summer, 1937. © Arktisk Institut (CJB3032). Photo by Jette Bang.

∼ TRADING SEALSKINS LONG AGO

We visited the trading post even with one sealskin to sell. The price of a sealskin with fur removed was fifty cents. I think sealskins with fur still on was twenty-five cents. A pair of bearded sealskin boots were traded for only $2.00. You could sell a pair of sealskin boots with fur, or waterproof ones without fur, for different prices. I also remember getting a dollar and a half for a pair of waterproof furless sealskin boots, and $1.25 for a winter pair with fur.

Peter Stone, Kuujjuaraapik, Quebec, Avataq Cultural Institute

In the mid-1950s, the Hudson's Bay Company began to buy sealskins from the hunters, allowing seal hunting to be a self-supporting endeavor. A few years later, however, protests against the harp seal hunt in eastern Canada began—a hunt that has nothing to do with the Inuit subsistence hunt. The anti-sealing campaign gained steam in the 1970s, when French film star Brigitte Bardot joined the fray, visiting the ice off Newfoundland, having her photograph taken with a baby whitecoat seal pup, and thus attracting a lot of attention for the animal rights movement. In 1983 the European Community banned harp and hooded seal imports, and the market for all sealskin products completely collapsed. It has yet to recover.

The result was that an Inuk hunter who had sold his sealskin byproduct for $23 in 1976—before Brigitte Bardot's appearance on the ice off Newfoundland and in heart-rending photographs across Europe—suddenly found that the same skin was worth less than $4. In 1976, Inuit across northern Canada had sold 63,000 sealskins, producing enough cash income to support their subsistence

hunting for seals and other game. Equally important, the seals—mostly adult ringed seals—harvested by Inuit hunters provided 1.5 million kilograms of meat for their families. To purchase that much food, imported from southern Canada, would mean a cost of about $15 million to feed Inuit families collectively. The next year, with virtually no market for the sealskins, many Inuit could not afford to hunt. In 1976, it cost a hunter about $7000 to equip himself and operate for a year—he would have to sell about 300 ringed seal skins to offset that cost of harvesting food for his family. That was probably an unreachable goal, but earning a good portion of the $7000 from selling the sealskins was not an unreasonable proposition. Ten years later, the same hunter's costs had doubled and it was almost impossible to sell sealskins. Today, for a hunter to be adequately equipped, it costs even more, and income levels among Canada's Inuit are simply not high enough for the majority to continue a hunting lifestyle. In a few short years, the animal rights movement had effectively destroyed Inuit hunters' only (at the time) hope of self-sufficiency. By the mid-1980s, the number of seal pelts exported annually from Canada's North had fallen by 97 percent from its peak ten years earlier.

With the collapse of the sealskin market, social assistance payments to Canadian Inuit have risen dramatically, as have rates of suicide, domestic violence, and substance abuse. The anti-sealing campaign has changed life in the North forever.

Ali Ippak

⌒ THE EUROPEAN BAN
ON SEALSKIN IMPORTS

I really don't know, but the only way to have people start buying skins again is to have them understand. I guess it is the only way. As Inuit we do not count how many seals we are going to catch during any period of time. We put a lot of effort into trying to catch seals, and some days we do not catch any, other days several, some days just one. They should be made to understand that it is so difficult for us. They, on the other hand, claim that seals are being killed off. The selling of sealskins stopped because of their opposition to the massive killing of seals. We are not like that. I've said this because I think sealskins could be sold again.

ALI IPPAK, BORN 1947, SANIKILUAQ, NUNAVUT
TRANSLATED BY QILUQQI

Why was the effect on Inuit so devastating? The seal hunt, for Inuit, was never just a matter of harvesting food. With whom a man hunted, how the food was shared, and how decisions were

FACING PAGE

Women sewing sealskins for an *umiaq*, Ivujivik, northern Quebec, 1960.

Canadian Museum of Civilization

(J6497). Photo by Eugene Arima.

made were all important elements of the process. The seal hunt was woven into an entire matrix of social values, and the end of the hunt meant the end of a way of life.

Outside of Canada, the effect of Europe's import ban on seal products was less dramatic, for various reasons. In Alaska, for example, the Inuit were much less dependent on the sealskin trade, having already become involved in oil and gas development. In northern Norway, the harp seal hunt was already in decline. And in Greenland, the Home Rule government responded to the ban decisively and effectively by introducing national subsidies on the purchase of sealskins from hunters.

Recently there have been efforts to reestablish a market for seals in Canada. The economic development corporation formed by Inuit of Baffin Island as a result of the Nunavut land claim is looking for offshore buyers of by-products from the subsistence seal hunt, which could provide a steady market for seal hunters. In 1999 the annual fur auction held in North Bay, Ontario, included sealskins for the first time. Seal oil is a rich source of an Omega-3 fatty acid that prevents thrombosis and atherosclerosis, and there is now a growing industry to render seal oil and sell it in capsule form to health-conscious consumers all over the world. As a result of these initiatives, as well as a movement to ease restrictions on seal imports into Europe and the United States, seals may once again be able to resume their place at the heart of the Inuit economy.

But the importance of the seal to Inuit extends far beyond its economic value. The seal lies at the foundation of traditional Inuit society, the complex of material, social, spiritual, and cultural values that define for many Inuit who they are.

Rebirth

THAT DAY in March in Cambridge Bay comes to mind once again. The land is covered with snow, the sea solidly frozen, yet a hint of spring is in the air. A sun dog sparkles overhead. For Analok, the scene is full of meaning. He travels back in time to his youth as he gazes beyond the window, back to a cluster of iglus on the windswept sea ice not far from where the village now stands. His people no longer live on the land, where life was a fusion of all he now sees—the snow and ice, the sky and the annual cycle of the sun—but he knows that his people remain as strong as the beliefs that have sustained them for generations in that environment. Gazing out the window, Analok seems to look beyond the real world to where the great spirits dwell. There the powers of Nuliajuk, the Mother of the Sea, and those of Sila, who controls the wind and weather, and Tatqiq, the spirit of the sky, merge with the soul of a wise old Inuk. On that bright March day, perhaps Analok can see and feel them all, and the single thought that brings them into focus for him as he studies the sun dog's magic light is, yes, it is today that the new seals are to be born so that our lives may continue.

Frank Analok

OVERLEAF

Two Inuit hunters in seal-skin kayaks near the mouth of the Mackenzie River, western Canadian Arctic, ca. 1914. Kenneth Gordon Chipman collection, National Archives of Canada (c5106). Photo by C. W. Mathers

$\mathcal{A}$ CKNOWLEDGMENTS

IT WOULD BE an impossible task to name all the people around the circumpolar world who have contributed over the years to my understanding of seals from the perspective of those who know them best. I especially want to acknowledge Analok and Ekvanna in Cambridge Bay, Sikkuark in Kugaaruk, Mikitok in Coral Harbour, and Peter Irniq in Iqaluit, all of them friends and advisers as well as informants to this work. I am grateful to each of them in many inexpressible ways. The knowledge contained in these pages comes from them and from a host of others, too numerous to list, in Alaska, Nunavut, Nunavik, Greenland, Norway, and Russia. The strength of this book, I hope, is that it is based directly on the traditional knowledge of these people, whose lives depended on that knowledge.

There are many other organizations and individuals who helped to make this book a reality, some in tangible ways, others in intangible ways—both important and equally appreciated. For their assistance, I would like to acknowledge the following: *Above & Beyond* magazine, Air Inuit, the Avataq Cultural Institute, First Air, the Igloolik Research Centre, the Inuit Tapirisat of Canada, the Kitikmeot Heritage Society, the Nunavut Research Institute, Taqramiut Productions Inc., Frank Analok, Mabel Angulalik, Martha Angulalik, Irina Appa, Piera Balto, Terje Brantenberg, Mikitok Bruce, Jane Claricoates, Holly Cleator, Sylvie Côté-Chew, Kim Crockatt, Bill Doidge, Leonie Duffy, James Eetoolook, Flemming Enequist, Attima Hadlari, Keith Hay, Jorgen Hodal, Peter Horsman, Roy Inglangasuk, Stuart Innes, Peter Irniq, Akatu Paaviaaraq Jakobsen, Amalie Jessen, Margo Kadlun, Brendan Kelly, Bill Kemp, Tom Koelbel, Kit Kovacs, Joanne Logan, Dominic Lynch, John Macdonald, Miriam McDonald, Ken MacRury, Ian Moir, Gert Mulvad, Joe Netser, Frances Pelly, Laurie Pelly, Lynn Peplinski, John Poirier, Yngvar Ramstad, Peggy Roe, Kate Sanderson, Candace Savage, Svavar Sigmundsson, Nick Sikkuark, Doug Stern, Rob Stewart, Manitok Thompson, Lisa Uqaituk, George Wenzel, and Darlene Wight. Others, more numerous, whose information is directly quoted, are cited throughout the text.

Furthermore, I am grateful for financial assistance received from the Government of the Northwest Territories Department of Resources, Wildlife and Economic Development, which helped with research costs, and from the Nunavut Arts Council.

To Rob Sanders, who had the vision to venture into uncharted territory, and to Nancy Flight, whose consummate patience and intelligence helped tranform my prose, and to Val Speidel for her harmonious design, I extend my sincerest gratitude. Both author and reader are fortunate that these three had a hand in the book.

Finally, I am indebted to my favorite companions out on the land, Ayalik and Laurie, for their enthusiasm, support, and understanding.

$\mathcal{B}$IBLIOGRAPHY

The richest and most important sources used in the writing of this book were the oral testimonies of Inuit in Canada, Alaska, and Greenland.

Balikci, Asen. *The Netsilik Eskimo.* New York: American Museum of Natural History Press, 1970.

Bonner, Nigel. *Seals and Man: A Study of Interactions.* Seattle: University of Washington Press, 1982.

———. *Seals and Sea Lions of the World.* New York: Facts on File, 1994.

Brandson, Lorraine E. *Carved from the Land: The Eskimo Museum Collection.* Churchill, Man.: Diocese of Churchill Hudson Bay, 1994.

Canada. Royal Commission on Seals and the Sealing Industry in Canada. *Seals and Sealing in Canada: Report of the Royal Commission.* Vols. 1–3. Ottawa: Minister of Supply and Services Canada, 1986.

Condon, Richard. *The Northern Copper Inuit: A History.* Toronto: University of Toronto Press, 1996.

Freeman, Milton M.R., Eleanor E. Wein, and Darren E. Keith. *Recovering Rights: Bowhead Whales and Inuvialuit Subsistence in the Western Canadian Arctic.* Edmonton: Canadian Circumpolar Institute and Fisheries Joint Management Committee, 1992.

Jenness, Diamond. *Report of the Canadian Arctic Expedition, 1913–18.* Ottawa: 1923.

Lavigne, David M., and Kit Kovacs. *Harps and Hoods: Ice-Breeding Seals of the Northwest Atlantic.* Waterloo, Ont.: University of Waterloo Press, 1988.

McLaren, I.A. *The Biology of the Ringed Seal in the Eastern Canadian Arctic.* Bulletin 118. Ottawa: Fisheries Research Board of Canada, 1958.

Murdoch, John. *Ethnological Results of the Point Barrow Expedition.* Washington, D.C.: Smithsonian Institute Press, 1988.

Nelson, Richard K. *Hunters of the Northern Ice.* Chicago: University of Chicago Press, 1969.

Oakes, Jill, and Rick Riewe. *Spirit of Siberia: Traditional Native Life, Clothing, and Footwear.* Vancouver: Douglas & McIntyre, 1998.

Rasmussen, Knud. *Intellectual Culture of the Iglulik Eskimos.* Vol. 7 (1) of *Report of the Fifth Thule Expedition 1921–24.* Copenhagen: Gyldendalske Boghandel, Nordisk Forlag, 1929.

———. *The Netsilik Eskimos: Social Life and Spiritual Culture.* Vol. 8 (1, 2) of

Report of the Fifth Thule Expedition 1921–24. Copenhagen: Gyldendalske Boghandel, Nordisk Forlag, 1931.

Ridgwat, S. H., and R. J. Harrison. *Seals*. Vol. 2 of *Handbook of Marine Mammals*. London: Academic Press, 1981.

Roe, Peggy. "Sedna: The Myth of the Inuit Sea Goddess." Unpublished paper, 1996.

Ronald, K., and J. L. Dougan. "The Ice Lover: Biology of the Harp Seal." *Science* 215 (1982): 928–33.

Smith, Thomas G. *The Ringed Seal*, Phoca hispida, *of the Canadian Western Arctic*. Ottawa: Department of Fisheries and Oceans, 1987.

Spencer, Robert F. *The North Alaskan Eskimo: Study in Ecology and Society*. Washington, D.C.: Smithsonian Institute Press, 1959; Toronto: General Publishing , 1976.

Stewart, R. E. A., et al. *Seals and Sealing in Canada's Northern and Arctic Regions*. Winnipeg: Department of Fisheries and Oceans, 1986.

Traill-Dennison, Walter. *Orkney Folklore and Sea Legends*. Orkney, U.K.: Orkney Press, 1994.

Wenzel, George. *Animal Rights, Human Rights*. Toronto: University of Toronto Press, 1991.

West, John F. *Faroese Folk-Tales & Legends*. Lerwick, Scotland: Shetland Press, 1980.

Weyer, E. M. *The Eskimos: Their Environment and Folkways*. New Haven, Conn.: Yale University Press, 1932.

INDEX

Seal hunters. *See* Hunters, Inuit

Seal hunting, prehistoric, 6–7

Seal hunting by kayak, 87, 88, 89, 98, 99, *100–101*

Seal lairs, 79, 83, 86, *86*

Seal liver, 56, *57*, 66, 72, 105

Seal meat

  cooking of, 26, 31, 40, 105

  distribution of, 24, 56, 62, 66–67, 68, 72, 87

  historic use in Iceland, 6

  and Inuit diet, 109, 112

  parts eaten by men and women, 72

  and the Sami, 7

  and taboos, 26, 40

Seal oil, 6, 37, 64, 80, 114

Seal oil lamp

  as source of heat and light, ix, 36, 40, 64, 68, 82, 105

  and taboos, 70, 71

  uses of, ix, 64

Seal populations, 1, 2, 4, 91

Seal pups, 79, 86, 91, 94, 110

Seals, Arctic

  about, 53, 78, 87

  butchering of, x, 28, 31, 56, 67

  carvings of, *xii–xiii, 29, 30, 73*

  as central to survival, xii, 1, 7, 12, 33, 38, 82, 89

  circumpolar peoples' use of, 1, 5–9

  and currents, 53

  and Inuit, 5, 9, 89, 109, 114, 115

  killing of, 11, 54

  numbers harvested, 1, 94, 98, 112

  and transformation, 12, 15, 18, 20–24

  types of, 1–2

  See also names of seals

Sealskin(s)

  market for, 110, 112, 114

  preparation of, viii–ix, *61*, 70, *110–11*

  and the Sami, 7

  trading of, 7–8, 110

  use of, 1, 6

Sealskin boats. *See* Kayaks; *Umiat*

Sealskin boots, ix, 2, 7, 88, 110

Sealskin clothing, ix, 7, 88, 89, 99, 109

Sealskin floats, 80, *81*, 89

Sealskin rope, *41*, 43, *44*, 54, 88

Seal skulls, 64, 66

Seal souls/spirits, 21, 64, 66, 71

Seal teeth, 43

Sea scorpion, 43

Sedna, 11, *13*, *25*. *See also* Mother of the Sea; Nuliajuk; Takanaluk; Taleelayuk

Selkies, 20–21, *22–24*

Sewing, viii–ix, 40, 56, 60, 71, *112*

Shamans, ix, *10*, 20, 26

Sharing, 37, 64, 66–67, 72, 87, 106

Shetland Islands, 18, 20

Sila (spirit), 115

Sinews, 71, 86

Sleds, *34–35, 36–37, 47, 56–57,* 99

Snow, for drinking water, 45–46, 64

Snowhouses. *See* Iglus

Snowknife, 43, 45

Snowmobiles, 99, 109

Soapstone carvings. *See* Carvings, stone

Soapstone oil lamp. *See* Seal oil lamp

Souls, animal, 31, 106

Spirit helpers, ix, *30*

Spirits, ix, 11, 26, 70, 115

  animal, appeasement of, ix, x, 21, 60

  sea, carvings of, *10, 14, 25*

  sea, illustrations of, *12–13, 19*

Spiritual practices. *See* Rituals; Shamans

Spotted seals, 4

Spring, 46, 53, 82

  behavior of seals in, 72, 78–79

  as time seals are born, 9, 115

  See also Seal hunt, spring

Starvation, 104

Stone, Peter, 110

Success in the hunt

  and acceptance, 56

  and hunters, 54, 68

  and respect, ix, 27, 54, 106

  and shamans, ix, 26

  in spring, 82

  and survival, 27, 33

Sun dog, 9, 115

Survival

  hunting as basis of, 106

  seals as central to, 1, 7, 12, 33, 38, 82, 89

  and success in the seal hunt, 27, 33

**FIRST NATIONS
HOUSE OF LEARNING**

**XWI7XWA
LIBRARY**